MY CREEPY PARANORMAL STORY

SCARY STORIES INSPIRED BY REAL ENCOUNTERS WITH GHOSTS, CREATURES, AND THE UNKNOWN

DAVE HANN & H.J. TIDY

Contents

Introduction v

Chapter 1: Cabin Encounter 1

Chapter 2: Not Alone 11

Chapter 3: Texter 21

Chapter 4: Dad's Painting 33

Chapter 5: Lady in White 43

Chapter 6: Grandma's Doll 53

Chapter 7: Shack in the Woods 63

Chapter 8: Tell Me Your Name 71

Chapter 9: The Neighbor 81

Chapter 10: Classified 91

Chapter 11: Lonely Cabin 99

Conclusion 107

Introduction

According to the godfather of weird fiction, H. P. Lovecraft, the greatest fear is the fear of the unknown. We all know that. We've had that feeling when we experience something we can't explain. It's that gnawing, gut-wrenching, physical fear that comes from our desire to know, and at the same time, not to know. Maybe knowing would be worse than not knowing.

That's why we try to explain to ourselves what is happening. We never think that's a ghost. We try to explain things, to make ourselves feel better, to make ourselves believe that the world is still ordinary. Sometimes, we fail.

Many years ago, I was living in an old house that had been divided into two. The original house was probably a hundred years or so old. My apartment was relatively small, the ideal place for a university student. It had a tiny kitchen, a tiny bathroom, a lounge with lovely old wood paneling, and a small bedroom with a built-in wardrobe. While I was comfortable, I did find that the apartment never seemed to have enough light. Every room except the kitchen seemed filled with shadows.

While it might sound like an ideal haunted house, I never had any weird experience there—except for one night. I woke up in the middle of the night, probably about one or two in the morning. At first I didn't know why I'd woken, but then I heard an odd sound, something that made no sense to me. It sounded like tapping or scratching coming from the wardrobe. I lay there, wondering what was happening, and feeling, at the very least, uncomfortable. I tried to figure out what could be making the sounds. Insects? Mice? Wind? Nothing seemed quite right.

I tried to ignore it, but that didn't work. I couldn't go back to sleep. I tried to convince myself it was normal, but somehow I just couldn't make myself believe that. By this time, I admit, I was getting a bit creeped out by the experience. A large part of me just wanted to hide under the covers and stay there till sunrise. At the same time, though, I wanted to sleep. I'm still unsure why I did it, maybe just out of sheer frustration, but I decided I had to make this stop. I screwed up my courage, and then loudly and clearly, I said, "cut that out!"

The noise stopped, just like that. Cut off in an instant. I was never bothered by any more noises or odd experiences in that apartment. What caused the noise, and why it stopped, I have no idea. Yet I needed an explanation, so I rationalized it as mice. I'd scared them away. Yet, I never saw any sign of mice in the wardrobe or in the apartment itself.

Oddly enough, I've never actually told anyone that story before. I think that's true for most of us. If we have a strange experience, we tend to keep it to ourselves. We don't want people thinking we're weird or crazy. And, maybe, if we don't talk about it, it won't seem so real. We can just write it off as a dream or something. For the record, I was wide awake that night.

Luckily for us, not everyone wants to keep their stories to themselves. This book, and Night Terror Publishing, intend to get stories of the weird and spooky out of hiding and into the hands of readers. Night Terror Publishing is all about taking those strange stories, be they about the paranormal, true crime, or strange disappearances, and presenting them for you, the reader. This anthology you are holding or looking at on a device is just that, a selection of events that happened to other people and, luckily, not to you.

You see, all the stories in this book are real. H.J. Tidy asked his fellow readers, like you, through his social media platforms and email newsletters, to share their weird and spooky experiences. They did, and here are some of the stranger ones that got sent in. These are the stories that people like you sent.

That's not to say the stories happened as they are written here. We did, at times, use some dramatic license. After all, you bought this book to be entertained, chilled and taken away from the cares of the day. You came to this book to read a good spooky story and to have those icy fingers run down your spine, all the while knowing it's just a story. Well, these are stories, but not just stories. These are all based on happenings and events reported to H.J. Tidy. Names, places, and descriptions may have been changed, but not the story, not the main event. The plot, the core of the story, is what matters. We kept that. These stories are what people experienced, and this is what they told us happened. Now we're sharing that with you.

As a writer, this has been an enjoyable challenge. I enjoy writing horror and dark fantasy. I don't know why. Even if I try to write a happy story, it gets dark all by itself. I like the dark. I like the mystery. However, if you ask the students I teach at university, they'll tell you I'm an outgoing and relaxed guy (I hope). They are often surprised that I write what I do. So why do I like the dark? Maybe for the same reason you're reading this book—to enjoy that chill, that fear of what might be out there. There were a couple of stories here that had me looking behind me at times when I was reading them.

Remember, this time, these things are out there. These are not stories from my mind. These stories came to us from people who've experienced them, from people who reported these events to us. These are stories like the one I mentioned at the start about the strange noise in my wardrobe, only a lot creepier. That means that, unlike many books of weird stories, there are often no tidy endings, no clean wrap-ups. These events are real-life, messy, unpredictable, and sometimes downright spooky. Events can suddenly impact the most ordinary of people. The strange—the weird—can unexpectedly pop up out of nowhere.

Like, for example, the time I was walking back one night from my parents-in-law's house. Something attracted my attention to the sky. In the darkness, a single red light was drifting past. It made no noise, just glowed its way across the pitch dark sky. A plane, I assumed, despite the lack of noise.

Planes, though, don't just have red lights. They're not silent. They don't come in groups. More red lights started drifting across the sky, all silent. I looked to the left, to the right, there they were, just little pinpoints of red, floating past. I felt that feeling then. That feeling that something has happened to take you out of the ordinary world, to put you into a world of magic and downright weirdness. There's a unique mix of fear, wonder, and awe. Reality has changed, and you don't know how much.

What happened next? Well, I might tell you later, because, honestly, this book is not about me. This book is about the people who sent in their stories and the strange events that happened to them.

These people have told us about a lot of things. We certainly appreciate them taking the time to send in their stories. Here you'll find stories of ghosts, monsters that you were sure didn't exist, of aliens, of apparently everyday items that seem to have an evil presence around them. There are houses with almost traditional ghosts and homes that seem determined to control the people in them. There are things in the wild that are not human and not animals either. There are things out there that are frightening.

Settle down in a comfortable spot, and make sure to leave all the lights on because here are the stories of real people confronting real events with real fear.

Chapter 1
Cabin Encounter

I was frozen, totally unable to move. I wanted to. My mind was shouting in my head, begging me to move, but while it was staring into my eyes, I couldn't. Then it took a step toward me.

My uncle has a cabin in northern California, up in the Cascades about ten miles south of Mount Shasta. It's up a dirt road, TV Road or Microwave Road, or something like that. It's in the middle of nowhere, or, really, in the middle of a forest.

I used to go up there when I was a kid and well into my teen years. I loved it. I have many fond memories of that forest. I used to laugh at the people who went on vacations to fancy resorts. How is it a vacation with all those other people surrounding you? Up in the woods, you can really get away from the crowds and all the hassles of civilization.

A couple of years ago, my Grandma called me and asked if I'd like to go up to the cabin for a week. Apparently, my uncle needed to go into the hospital for an operation—nothing big, no need to worry. He wanted someone to go out to the cabin and look after it, along with his dog.

Well, I was in college, and it was summer break, so yeah. I jumped at the idea. I asked Grandma if I could bring a friend with me, and she hemmed and hawed a bit until I told her it was another girl from my class. She was fine with that. I think she was worried I'd be bringing a boy up for a "fun" weekend. She's a bit old-fashioned like that.

Carol and I flew into Sacramento in the morning, and Grandma picked us up. Now my Grandma may be a bit old-fashioned about some things, but she does love to drive fast. We were up at the cabin in time for lunch, and that counts stopping at Trader Joe's in Redding for supplies.

The cabin was pretty much as I remembered it: a two-story, blue, wooden building in a clearing just off the "road." It had a wraparound porch and an old metal garage off to one side. Carol, who'd never been out of a big city in her life, seemed a bit nonplussed, but she'd been like that ever since we turned up the dirt road.

"Come on," I said. "It's great inside."

I was about to drag her inside when Grandma harrumphed at us. A bit shamefaced, Carol and I grabbed the supplies. Carol was still looking at the cabin a bit skeptically, but her face brightened when we got inside.

My uncle has always said it's not what's on the outside that matters. When it came to his cabin, he practiced what he preached. Once you got inside you realized what he meant. The living room has all-leather furniture and polished wood. The kitchen is really modern. The TVs take up half the wall in most rooms. Carol brightened up a lot once she saw the inside. I guess she'd been thinking we'd be roughing it.

Barney was happy to see us too. He's my uncle's dog. He's an old black Labrador. I have no idea how old. He doesn't move that fast anymore, but his tail still wagged at full speed when we untied him from the back porch and let him inside. My uncle says he has to stay off the furniture, but my uncle wasn't there, was he?

"Your uncle's redecorating the bedrooms," Grandma said, giving the dog on the sofa an evil look. "You two will have to sleep in his room. It's the only one that's livable right now."

I remembered my uncle's room. It was the one at the south end of the cabin, facing the woods at their thickest. I grabbed Carol's hand and pulled her upstairs.

"Ta-da," I said, swinging the door open.

The room was much as I remembered it. It was all wood paneling, a deer's head mounted over the dresser, and a huge iron bedstead with a big, soft, fluffy mattress.

Then I looked up at the windows. They'd been changed, the old wooden frames replaced by new aluminum ones. The windows also seemed to have been repositioned slightly. Where the big old window looking south had been, there was now a smaller one. The one on the west wall had been enlarged, better for evening sun, I guessed.

I walked over to the south window. The closer I got, the slower I walked. Something in my mind was telling me that I didn't like that window. I couldn't remember exactly why, but that window had some sort of bad memory attached to it. I pushed that away. I was an adult, a college post-grad. I had no time for childish fears.

I reached the window and looked through. There was the forest, as I remembered it. The sun was nearly vertical, casting shadows on the forest floor. There was nothing among the trees. I looked carefully. Now, why'd I do that? Why would there be something among the trees?

Carol came up beside me. "You okay?"

That snapped me out of it. "Yeah, fine. Thought ... something. Doesn't matter. Cool room, eh?"

She smiled. "Yeah, but very ... masculine."

I grinned too. "We'll just have to put up with that."

We went back downstairs. Grandma had lunch ready for us. Barney, I noticed, had been evicted from the sofa and was now on his mat.

We sat at the table and dug in. There's something about the country's fresh air that just makes you want to eat, diet or no diet.

"What do you think of the house, dear?" Grandma asked Carol.

Carol swallowed and replied. "It's great. Not at all what I expected from the outside. What's the deal with the window in Tatiana's uncle's room, though? She seemed a bit freaked by it."

Grandma thought for a few seconds and then grinned. "Ah, that will be Tatiana's hairy man."

"Huh?" was the best response I could come up with.

Grandma put on her storytelling face. "Don't you remember, dear? When we used to come up here with your mother, you'd go into your uncle's room and look out the old south-facing window. You'd come and tell us you could see some big hairy man out in the woods and drag your mother and me up to see. We never could see anything, and I never understood why you just didn't take us out to the back porch. You always were a bit odd as a child, saying you saw things that no one else could. Like the little gray men at the bottom of the field that one day at Black Butte. A vivid imagination, I think, and one that you seem to have grown out of."

I blushed a bit at that, but it did bring back memories. I used to go into my uncle's room when I was younger and look

4

at the forest. It was so close and so thick. Sometimes, I'd see something out there. Among the trees would be a figure, tall, taller than my father, and covered in dark reddish-brown fur. I never knew what to make of it. My uncle is a teaser. He loves to wind people up. I thought he might have set up something in the woods to scare me. Mostly it didn't.

It always bothered me, though, that whenever I managed to get my mom and my Grandma upstairs to look, it was gone. I would look out with them and could never see it. It was like it was only there when I was looking alone. And, no, it was not my imagination. It was real, I swear.

Later in the afternoon, Grandma got in her car and disappeared down the track in a cloud of dust and stones. She'd left us the number of the nearest neighbor. He lived about 300 yards down the road, but the forest was so thick you'd never know it.

We fed Barney, watched some TV, and then headed upstairs to bed for the night. My uncle's bed is so huge that there was plenty of room for both of us.

As we settled in, Carol asked, "Did you really see a Bigfoot out there?"

"I don't know what it was," I replied, lying on my back. I explained how I thought it might have been something my uncle dreamed up.

"There's more, though, isn't there?" Carol pushed. She knew me so well.

I rolled over and looked straight at her. "Yes. There was one afternoon, late in the day. I'd pulled Mom and Grandma up here again, and we'd seen nothing. They left, laughing at me. I was about fourteen at the time and not happy at being laughed at. I stayed here, my eyes just above the window ledge, watching the forest.

"I don't know how long I stayed like that, the whole thing is a bit hazy, but I saw it come back. It poked its head around one of the big trees out there. I was angry. I stayed crouching there, staring at it, loathing it. God, I hated it. Why wouldn't it come out when other people were in the room?"

I trailed off, and Carol prompted me again. "Is that all?"

I was struggling with my memories. Some things seemed clear, but a lot didn't make sense.

"I don't know," I said. "Honestly, the whole thing gets real vague and weird about then."

"Tell me," she said quietly. "Tell me whatever you remember."

I rolled on my back again, trying to clear the fuzz from my mind. "It saw me. It must have. It faced the window, looked up at me. I saw its face ... almost human ... eyes, bright, staring. I was so angry. I just stared back.

"Then, it moved. It moved away from the trees. It headed for the back porch. It wasn't moving fast, just loping, almost casually, and never breaking with my gaze. I broke. I ran. I ran so fast to find my family, to warn them ..."

"And?" Carol asked, engrossed.

I concentrated, but nothing came. "That's the weird part. I can't remember. I remember running out the bedroom door, down the hall, but then ... nothing. The next thing I can remember is that we had a barbecue that night. No Bigfoot, no scary hairy man, no mention of it."

Carol pulled her side of the blanket up tighter. "Jeez, weird."

I shook my head, trying to clear the fluff out of my brain. "Yeah" was the best I could offer.

"And that thing was just out there?" she asked. In the glow of the nightlight, I could see her hand waving in the direction of the south window.

"Yes, but that was years ago. My uncle's been up here for years and never said anything about any Bigfoot. Maybe I dreamed it." Thinking that way made me feel better, safer, more secure.

"Mmm," said Carol. "I'm going to find it hard to sleep tonight."

"I'm not," I said, scrunching down under the covers. It was true. Whatever memories I had were already fading again, replaced by the comfort of the soft bed and a good friend. I drifted off almost immediately.

I can't say much happened the next day. I know I slept in late and did, well, pretty much nothing. Barney really took almost no looking after. He was so grateful to be allowed on the sofa that he'd just stay there and pretend to sleep. Maybe he was like a child; if I don't look at you, you won't look at me—and kick me off the sofa.

I was restless that night. Carol had already gone up to the room, but I couldn't settle. I'd had a shower but was still in no mood to head to bed. Instead, I grabbed a soda and walked outside.

It was a beautiful night. The sky was clear, and the half-moon and stars bathed the clearing around the cabin in soft light. I inhaled deeply, letting the cool crisp night air fill my lungs. It seemed to relax me.

I walked off the porch, leaned my back against the rail. The tension, the restlessness seemed to fade away, and I was about to head back to our room.

Then I heard a noise. There was a rustling among the trees. Idly I looked at the tree line, about 8 feet from the cabin. I couldn't see anything moving.

Then the rustling came again, followed by heavy thuds. The thuds seemed to be getting louder, faster, approaching, like the footsteps of something unusually heavy. I froze, unsure what to do. It sounded like an elephant running through the forest. My heart thumped almost as loudly as the footfalls. My palms suddenly felt damp. The tension that had vanished only a moment before returned in full force. What was coming?

Then it came out of the woods. It was the same shape I remembered from my youth: tall, man-shaped, covered in dark fur. My thoughts were muddled, confused. It's a person. My uncle's back playing tricks. It's not a person. It's too big. It came out of the forest. Something is wrong. It's not right. I remember … I froze, not wanting to draw attention to myself.

It didn't help. The thing looked my way. Its eyes locked with mine, somehow, even in the semi-darkness of the evening. I froze. I couldn't move. I felt paralyzed. I felt my own will had vanished, replaced by an overwhelming command to stay still, stay there. I felt like a gazelle in a TV documentary, being stared down by a lion.

There was more, though. Thoughts, memories flooded through my head. Everything that had happened to me in the past, all the strange things, they made sense. I didn't like it, however. I felt that my role in those events had not been voluntary or happy.

It took a step toward me. I felt my fear rise even higher. My heart was beating faster than I could ever remember. I could feel the adrenaline flooding my blood, but still I couldn't move. My mind was screaming for me to run. Run now! Not again. Get away! But I couldn't. I was rooted to the spot. Just a few feet from the door, and safety, I couldn't move.

I heard the window above me open and Carol's voice. "Tatiana? You out there?"

The thing looked up. As soon as its eyes left mine, I felt my control return. My muscles, primed and charged, powered me onto the porch and through the back door. I slammed it behind me, throwing the bolt. I refused to look out and see if it was still there. It scared me too much, and I had no desire to meet its gaze again.

I grabbed my phone, rang the neighbor, begged, pleaded for him to come and take us away. I screamed at Carol to grab our stuff. We were leaving.

He arrived a few minutes later. He said he couldn't see anything outside the cabin, but I was in no mood for discussion. We left. I was shaking so bad I couldn't even put the seatbelt on. Carol had to do that for me. I did remember to call Barney, though. I wasn't leaving him alone with ... whatever it was.

Grandma arrived the next morning. She took one look at me and said she'd take Carol, me, and Barney back to Sacramento. On the trip back, in the light of day, she asked me about the experience. I told her everything I remembered. To her credit, she listened, and she didn't judge. There was no comment about an overactive imagination this time.

She asked me what I remembered when I looked into the thing's eyes. That's when I hit the wall. I remember remembering, but I don't remember what those memories were. It is so frustrating. It's like I have the answer to everything that happened to me, but I can't remember it. I just remember that I once knew it.

These days I don't take vacations in the woods. These days I like resorts. I want to be surrounded by lots of people.

Chapter 2
Not Alone

The kitchen was empty. There was no one there or in the whole house. Then the plate started to vibrate, to move by itself. Sophia couldn't move. She stood stock-still, hypnotized by the movement.

Sophia is, for a good reason, too emotionally connected to write this story herself. She tried a couple of times, but she just couldn't get through it. Every time she attempted it, she'd just end up crying in the corner of the room or hiding under the bed. I felt that expressing herself would help her move on, so I agreed to write it for her, but on the understanding that I'd only take what she'd told me, or I heard from credible witnesses, and put it down for her, without any embellishment on my behalf.

So, here's Sophia's story.

Almost the whole of the story takes place one Saturday night about two months ago. Well, that's not entirely true. No event happens by itself, and there are always others that lead to it.

In Sophia's case, the initial event was a tragedy. Her father's death. It's a tragic story. Her father had drunk a bit too much one night and got into what Sophia describes as a "quarrel" with her mother. The argument scared Sophia. She went to her room and hid there. She heard the door slam and the sound of her father's car taking off into the night. After a while, she heard the police come to talk to her mother.

Her father's anger and alcohol-fueled nighttime drive had been cut short when he impacted a truck carrying gas cylinders. The resulting fire had burned all involved beyond recognition, but it was pretty clear that it was Sophia's father's car, and he'd been driving.

Not long after the accident, Grace—that's Sophia's mother—felt it was time to sell the house. There were just too many reminders of her late husband everywhere she looked. Sophia agreed. A new start would help them both. Grace found a reasonably priced house on Newman Drive, right on the east side of town. Grace and Sophia moved in as soon as they could, desperate to shake the memories.

That's not to say that they felt the house was perfect—far from it. Both Sophia and Grace felt slightly uncomfortable in the home. They both reported feeling a bit "weird," like someone was watching them. It made them jumpy and unsettled. Both wrote the feeling off as just another effect of the recent death. A tragedy like that is enough to make anyone feel agitated.

The house itself was much larger than they needed for just the two of them. Grace had been in such a hurry to move that she'd taken the first reasonable place she could find. They didn't have many possessions, having gotten rid of much of the furniture that reminded them of Sophia's dead father. So, even though the house came with an extensive basement, they never used it. They had nothing to store in it, and both of them felt the basement was "uncomfortable." Neither liked being down there.

So, one Saturday, Sophia came back from volleyball practice late in the afternoon. I'd been encouraging her to get engaged in extra-curricular activities to help her move on. She found a note from her mother on the table saying that Grace was off visiting Sophia's grandmother. There was a meal ready for her, so she settled down to a night in, barely registering that this was the first night she'd spent alone in the new house.

Sometime later—she's not sure of the exact time—Sophia went to her room to watch a movie on her TV. The movie was not as interesting as she'd expected, and she was starting to drift off when she heard a noise.

She wasn't sure exactly what it was she heard, but she knew where it came from—beneath her, in the basement. It was the middle of the night. No one went into the basement at any time. Even if Grace had returned, she wouldn't be down there.

Sophia was frozen on her bed. She didn't know what to do. When the noise was not repeated, she started to relax. She had been half-asleep. The TV had been on. Obviously, it had not been a real noise. She'd imagined it.

She turned the TV off, planning to sleep. The silence was shocking. Without the TV noise, she felt that her hearing was suddenly enhanced. She strained to hear any noise in the house. She'd never realized how the noise of another person in the house could be so comforting.

Then there was a noise, a rattling, a clattering, like plates in an earthquake, or stones falling on concrete.

An earthquake, that's what it was, she decided. It was California, after all. But, there was no other noise, and she couldn't feel any movement.

The noise stopped. Sophia was tense. Her skin crawled. An earthquake, though, that's all. Might even explain the first sound. Earthquakes do weird things.

Then she heard the sound again. It would start, stop, and then start up again. She couldn't figure out where it was coming from. Below her, the basement? In the kitchen? In her mother's room? It seemed to move, but she could never be sure to where.

Sophia was shaking, desperate to crawl under the covers and just hope it all went away. She forced herself to think, to do something. Get control of yourself. Think, girl, what's happening?

She'd never been in the house alone at night before. Maybe some sort of noise in the pipes? The house settling? She'd heard that older homes could make all sorts of noises.

Then a louder rattle seemed to come from the hall, just outside her room. She almost shrieked. That was no pipe. Was it?

The noise moved on. Was there someone in the house with her? Surely not. This was a lovely, peaceful town. She'd always been told how lucky she was to live here, not further south in Los Angeles. But, there was the noise, again. From the kitchen, maybe?

Sophia was not the bravest person, and she knew that. She'd been through a lot recently. She really didn't want to leave her room. She just wanted to hide in her bed, but she knew she couldn't. She was alone in the house, and she had to do something.

She forced herself off the bed and stood, shaking, beside it. The noise seemed to rush down the hall again. She had to find out what it was, but she wasn't going out there unarmed. She stared around her room, seeking a weapon.

She settled on a small three-legged stool from in front of her dresser. Grasping it by one of the legs, she moved to her bedroom door. The noise, the rattle, whatever it was, seemed to be in the kitchen now. She tried to still her shaking hand and then turned the doorknob.

The door was wrenched from her hand and slammed open. Wind? But then, from behind her, she felt a rush of air, cold air, going in the opposite direction. It felt like someone had rushed past her. Someone cold.

She spun, waving the stool in front of her. There was no one there. Slowly she turned completely around, looking everywhere, hoping to see no one. No one around. There was no movement. Still, she felt chilled. She was shivering. Her whole body seemed ice-cold even though the July night was warm.

A noise. From the kitchen. Like the last rattle, but quieter, softer. Maybe a cat or something had gotten in?

Sophia flicked on the hall light, welcoming the glow. She advanced toward the kitchen, stool held protectively in front of her.

There was no noise in the kitchen now. Sophia stepped through the doorway and hit the light switch. The room looked normal. There was no dripping tap, no noisy cat, nothing out of place. Sophia sighed. There was no sign of any intruder.

Was she just hearing things? Confusing normal house noise? A glass of water would help, perhaps. Settle her nerves and that lump in her throat. She stepped toward the sink.

And stopped! A large serving plate beside the sink was vibrating, rocking back and forth. It was moving slightly, but enough for her to clearly see. Then it started to pick up speed, moving faster, rocking further. Mesmerized, petrified, Sophia could only stand and watch as the oscillations increased and sped up. Soon the plate was just a noisy, rattling blur.

Then it flew. It seemed to leap off the bench, flashing past her head, smashing into the wall behind her. The crash, louder than she expected, and the shards of china hitting her, broke the spell. She screamed. The stool fell from her hand, and she spun on her heel, racing back to her room.

She slammed the door closed. Locked it and retreated to the far side of the room, putting the bed between her and the door. She slid to the floor, hugging her knees to her chest. This was impossible. There was, what, something, out there. Something wrong in the house. If only her mother would come back soon. Her mother would know what to do. She knew that with the certainty that any young teenage girl would. Her mother would fix it. Her mother would be home soon. Please.

She says she lost track of time but guesses it was only about five minutes later when there was a gentle knock on her bedroom door. Her mother! It had to be. She leaped from the corner and raced for the door. Everything would be fine now, and her mother would know what to do.

Her body flooded with relief as she unlocked the door and swung it open. No one. The hall was empty. The light was off again, but there was certainly no one at her door.

Thinking her mother must be about, she tried to call her. All that came out was a hoarse whisper, "Mom?"

There was no reply from the darkened hall. She strained her ears to hear anything that might suggest her mother was back.

Then she heard something. Footsteps, running footsteps. Down the other end of the hall, padding lightly to the end, and down the stairs to the basement. Then the house seemed to shake as the basement door slammed.

Her mother wouldn't go down there. No way. Certainly not at night.

Slowly Sophia backed into her room. She gently swung the door closed, without a sound, and locked it again. Then she slid under her bed. Her eyes fixed on her door.

If only her mother were home. If only she could talk to her mother. Phone! Call her. Her phone was just out of reach, on the dresser.

Sophia felt she was in a nightmare. Her heart was racing, and her brain was screaming at her to stay hidden, stay under the bed, but … if she could call her mother … if she could talk to her mom.

Keeping her eyes on the door, she started to slide backward under the bed. Her heart seemed to stop, and she almost screamed when her foot hit something soft. Fearfully she looked back, only to see an old stuffed toy.

Finally, on the other side of the bed, she slowly raised herself, keeping an eye on the door, and scrabbled for her phone as soon as her hand grasped it. She dropped to the floor and slid under the bed again, always keeping an eye on the doorway.

It wasn't easy to bring the phone around to her face under the bed, but she managed it eventually and dialed her mother. No reply. Really? That was odd. Her mother would always pick up when it was Sophia calling. She tried again. Still nothing. She couldn't talk to her mother. Her mother might be anywhere. Where was she? Why wasn't she home? Sophia needed her.

A faint, rattling sound came to her ears. Oh God, was it back? Sophia could only think of one other option. She dialed the police.

"Someone, in the house," Sophia managed to whisper. "Noises. In the basement, maybe. I'm alone."

The operator was helpful and calm. She talked to Sophia, clearly and slowly, calming her a bit. The feeling that she was connected to another person was enough to, at least a little, lower Sophia's heart rate. The operator promised to send a car as soon as she could and then kept Sophia on the phone, encouraging her. She praised Sophia for hiding under the bed and insisted that Sophia remain there. The operator would stay on the line, keep in contact until the police arrived. Sophia was so grateful. She felt like a child who had been swept up into the arms of a parent.

The sound of cars pulling up the drive, the faint glow of red and blue lights through the closed curtains brought even more relief to Sophia. She sagged, her joints loosening from a tenseness she'd forgotten she'd been holding. She felt like a rag doll.

This time a soft female voice accompanied the knock on her door. "Sophia. Open the door, please. This is the police."

She slid out from under the bed, unlocked the door, and fell into the arms of a tall, blonde female officer. The last stress and fear slipped out of her as the officer picked her up and carried her out to a waiting police car.

Wrapped in a blanket, with a cup of hot chocolate, she waited while the police went through the house. The officer who had carried her out remained with her, giving Sophia an extra sense of warmth and security.

The officer's radio crackled, and she listened briefly before smiling at Sophia. "They've done a full search. There's no one in the house."

Then the radio crackled again, and the officer's expression changed. "Oh."

When the other officers came and explained what they'd found, Sophia couldn't handle it. She broke down totally, but I don't blame her. Anyone would have. I'm sure I would have. However, it does mean that I have to explain what happened without any real reference to Sophia's thinking. She's found it almost impossible to express herself in this part of the evening. I have to rely on the testimony of the police officers involved.

There were three of them that night, plus the female officer detailed to protect Sophia. Unlike what you see in the movies, they did not split up. They moved together through the house, covering each other in case there was an intruder.

They searched the ground floor and found it clear. After that, they moved into the basement. There was no one down there, and they were about to leave when Officer Rios noticed something unusual. Several travel bags were stacked in the basement corner, which they had been told was empty. The bags seemed to have attracted a large number of flies and had a distinctively coppery smell.

An examination disclosed what Rios suspected. The bags contained the dismembered remains of a middle-aged woman. Further investigation would reveal a necklace with a G, usually worn by Sophia's mother, Grace. An extensive analysis confirmed the identity.

Oddly, the fingerprints of Sophia's father were found on both the body and the bags.

Sophia admits that the days when all this was coming to light passed her in a blur. She has very little recollection of anything before her mother's funeral. With the night's events and the fact that a second tragedy followed so close on her father's supposed death, this is understandable. She is, however, left with a lot of unanswered questions.

Is her father really dead? There seems no doubt that he was driving the car that night, and his fingerprints on old bags are hardly evidence he survived, but what about his prints being on the body? Is he alive, or did some part of him blame his argument with his wife for his death and come back for revenge?

And what caused the noises in the house and the plate to fly at Sophia? Was there some malign supernatural force at work in the house that night? Sophia's theory, which seems to make her happier, is that her mother's spirit warned her, keeping her in her room and out of danger. For the time being, I have no desire to challenge that.

Sophia now lives with her last remaining relative, her grandmother.

When she was leaving today, I asked her if she'd had any more strange experiences now that she'd moved. She said that was something we could discuss in another session.

Chapter 3
Texter

This story is a little different from our usual stories. Whereas we usually get a single story from a reader, this one developed over a month in a series of emails between H.J. Tidy and the young lady in question. To best get the feel of the event, we have left the story in the form of the email exchanges between the two, so you can get the full effect of this situation. Here are these emails.

contact@n*******.com
Strange experience – mine
1 Message
Nicole.Rain <nicrain@********.com> November 11 2019
To: contact@n*******.com
Hi H.J. Tidy,

My friend Steffi told me you were looking for "spooky" stories. I don't know if you think this is spooky enough, but I'll tell you what happened.

A couple of days ago, I had some friends over to my place, guys I used to know in college. We had a few drinks and a smoke (but I was still pretty straight). Paul, my best friend from my college days, suggested that we try a Ouija board. We all had a bit of a giggle and figured that would be fun.

It didn't take long to write one up. You know the usual, the letters, the numbers, yes and no. I grabbed a shot glass from the kitchen, a clean one, that we could use as a planchette (that's the right word. I looked it up online).

We sat around and put a finger each on the glass. Then we tried the usual questions. Are you there? Is anyone there? Does anyone want to communicate with us? Nothing. Not a thing. The glass didn't even shiver.

Then I asked, what's your name? That's when the glass started to move. I swear, I had my finger just resting on it, and so did the others, but it moved. I think we were shocked for a couple of seconds, but then we started to laugh again. It was just like in the movies.

It started to spell a name: D – E – U – M – O. It was moving again when I stopped it and took the glass off the board. Something about this just made me feel wrong. I can't exactly describe it, but I guess I felt cold. Cold, and with a strange feeling in the pit of my stomach. Suddenly I didn't feel like laughing anymore. I really needed to stop it.

My friends, of course, asked me why I'd done that. I tried to explain, but they didn't seem to understand. None of them had felt cold. They laughed at me and told me I was silly, but I know what I felt, and I didn't like it.

We relaxed again, talking casually about something, but my mind wouldn't stay focused. I was glad when my friends left, but also a little uncomfortable. I live by myself. Nothing happened, though, and I slept well enough.

I thought you might like to hear my story. I hope it's useful for you.

Nicole Rain
nicrain@********.com
Re: Strange experience – mine
2 Messages
H.J. Tidy contact@n*******.com> November 12 2019
To: nicrain@********.com
Hi Nicole,

Thanks for your story. It does sound a bit weird. I wonder why you felt the way you did.

I'm not sure I can use that story. It is just your feeling. In some way, I'd like to know what the whole name it was going to spell out was, but maybe you were better off stopping it when you did. Thanks again. Let me know if you have any other strange experiences.

Say hi to Steffi for me.

H.J. Tidy
contact@n*******.com
Re: Re: Strange experience – mine
3 Messages
Nicole.Rain <nicrain@********.com> December 8 2019
To: contact@n*******.com
H.J. Tidy,

Something really strange happened last night. I want to tell someone. Maybe you can tell me what it means. Even if you can't, maybe it'll be good for your stories. I hope you can tell me what's going on, though. It really scared me.

Last night I was watching TV. It wasn't that interesting, so I was playing around with my phone too. It vibrated. I saw

I had a text. I didn't know the sender, though. It wasn't from one of my contacts.

The text said, "I see you, Nicole."

That made me a bit uneasy. I live in a small apartment on the second floor of an old house. I didn't see how anyone could see me, but I went over to the window and looked out. It was dark, but the street lights threw some light on the sidewalk outside. I couldn't see anyone out there. I closed the blinds and went back to my seat. I figured it was one of my friends being a bit silly, so I decided to reply.

I sent a text: "Who is this?"

The reply was almost instant. "Just a friend. Someone who is watching."

Now I knew it wasn't a friend I knew well. The number was not in my contacts. I was feeling a bit confused. Maybe it was an older friend I'd deleted ages ago or someone using a different phone. But, no one I knew texted like this. I thought I'd try again to find out.

I replied, "Who are you?"

Again, the reply came almost as soon as I'd hit send. "I live here too!"

I was trying to understand that, maybe someone in one of the other apartments, when my phone pinged again. The new text read, "Are you enjoying watching TV?"

I almost dropped the phone. How could they know what I was doing? The blinds were closed. No one could see in. The only way they could know was if they were in here, with me. I looked around the room, but there was no one. I got up and went through the whole apartment. There was no one in it except me, and the doors were locked. I was starting to feel nervous. This situation was just a bit too weird. I decided to take control.

"Tell me who you are, or I will report this number to the police," I sent back.

There was no immediate reply. I relaxed. I'd given whoever it was a good scare. That'd teach them, trying to scare me like that.

Then the phone pinged again. I didn't want to look at it, but I thought it might be whoever it was telling me its name, and we could have a good laugh over their prank.

It wasn't.

The new text read, "Good luck with that. I'm standing right beside you. But no one will ever find me."

My head snapped from side to side. Obviously, there was no one there. I couldn't help feeling that someone was watching me, though. I started to get that feeling that I was being watched. My spine was crawling, and I wanted to back into a corner, where it felt safe.

I pulled myself together. No way was this ... whoever it was on the phone ... was going to scare me that easily. The apartment has a landline phone. I don't use it much, but I decided this was a good time to. If I used the landline, they wouldn't know it was me calling. They'd pick up, and I could tell them, clearly and in no uncertain terms, exactly what I thought of their silly prank.

I went to the kitchen counter, still feeling like I was being watched. I dialed. That's when I honestly got a shock. It went straight to the "number not in service" message. That was impossible. The number was definitely in service. It kept texting me.

I put the handset back and stared at my mobile phone. I was mesmerized, fascinated by what was going on. I just stood there and waited. Somehow I knew this was not over.

The phone pinged. I looked down at the screen, and the same number appeared. The message would have seemed non-threatening to most people. It simply said,

"I like your new haircut. It makes you look younger."

When I read that, I backed into a corner. I was looking all around me, looking at an empty apartment.

You see, that morning I'd had my hair cut. I don't post things like that online. I'm not into all that "look at me" stuff. The only people who would have known were my parents, who I'd seen that afternoon, or someone who knew me well and could see me now.

Family. Parents. Of course. They were playing some silly joke on me. They'd seen my haircut, and they knew I liked to watch TV in the evenings. I was grinning when I rang my dad. The grin vanished when my father said it wasn't him or mom. He must have heard the stress and fear in my voice because he promised he'd be over as soon as he could. When I hung up the phone, I felt even more alone. It would take him at least an hour to get to my place from theirs outside the city.

I looked at my mobile phone again. It was lying on the counter, apparently harmless, but I felt wrong just looking at it. Any second, I felt, it would ring again. I was scared. I had no idea what was happening or why. Someone was sending me messages, someone who could see me. Someone who didn't want to give me their name. Somehow them knowing me, and me not knowing them, gave them power over me. I had to do something.

I rang the police. When the operator answered, I broke down. I started sobbing, explaining between sobs what was happening. She was very nice, ensuring that I had done the obvious, locked the doors and windows, and checked for intruders. She promised that a car would be around as soon as it could. When I hung up from that call, I was feeling so much better. The operator had been a great comfort, and the promise of a visit from the police made me feel that things were under control.

Then my phone pinged.

The message was from the same number. It read, "Why did you have to do that?"

Then it got personal. The messages kept coming. I've screenshot all the messages that came up to this point. But they started to get insulting and personal after that. I'm not going to tell you what it sent. It's insulting and embarrassing. I'm sure you understand, H.J. Tidy.

These messages went on for ages. Message after message, almost too fast for me to read, and that's the strange thing. I felt I had to read every one. It never occurred to me to turn the phone off or ignore it. I was glued to that little screen, feeling physically sick as the profanity rolled down it.

When the stream of abuse stopped, it was an almost physical shock. I gasped and leaned back from the counter. I looked at the clock. A whole forty-five minutes had gone past. I hadn't noticed.

I took a couple of deep breaths, trying to slow my heart rate.

The phone pinged again.

I looked. "Nobody is going to help you!"

That made me look around again. I swear, there was no one in the room, but I couldn't help that feeling that someone was watching me.

The phone pinged.

With a growing sense of dread, I looked at the screen.

"I'll show you, you BITCH!"

I was starring at that when there was a loud banging on my door. I leaped into the air. I tried, not really successfully, to stifle a scream. There was another loud banging on the door. With my heart beating so fast I thought it would shatter, I crept up to the pinhole on the door. Taking a deep breath, I looked through.

Two police officers stood on the other side. Oh, my God, the relief. I felt like a balloon deflating. The anxiety, the fear, it all flowed out of me.

I let them in, and they started, very professionally, to go through the apartment. Unfortunately, they could only tell me what I already knew. No one else was in the house, and there was no sign that anyone had broken in.

I showed them the texts, but they apologetically told me there was nothing they could do about that. Unless there was someone in the house, or someone standing outside threatening me, there was really no way they could help me. They suggested I turn the phone off, an idea which had never occurred to me. Promising to keep an eye on the building when they could, they left.

I put the phone down on my coffee table and sat in a chair, looking at it. It was silent. It's stayed that way. I didn't get any more texts that night. I don't know what happened.

My father arrived shortly after the police left. He did exactly what they did and came up with the same answer. No one was in the apartment. He did, however, point out some unusual looking scratch marks on the outside of the front door. It looked like something very hot had scratched the wood paneling. The marks were like burns running in threes. Again, I know I'd seen them when I'd come back to the apartment that afternoon, but for some reason, I ignored them. I don't understand why.

So, H.J. Tidy. That's what's happened to me. I don't know if it's connected to the other story I sent you. I don't know what's going on, but you did ask me to send you any new experiences. Well, that's it.

H.J. Tidy, if you can tell me what's going on, if you can tell me I'm not crazy, I'd love to hear it. Tell me something, H.J. Tidy. Help me out.

Nicole.
nicrain@********.com
Re: Re: Re: Strange experience – mine
4 Messages
H.J. Tidy <contact@n*******.com> December 9 2019
To: nicrain@********.com
Hello Nicole,

Thank you so much for sending such a detailed account. That's very helpful for me.

I wish I could tell you a bit more about your experience, but I don't know what to say. I'm sure you're not crazy. You have the phone messages to prove that. I know that dealing with the unknown can be stressful, but remember, nothing physical happened to you. You just got some strange and abusive texts from someone you didn't know. I think it would be better for you to think of them that way and not try to connect them to your other experience. Maybe get some friends over. Fill the apartment with happiness. Drive the bad memories away with good ones.

I'm not surprised you couldn't turn your phone off. I don't think any of us can these days. I certainly can't.

I'll talk to a couple of people about your experience, but don't worry about it. I'm sure it's over now.

Thanks again for keeping me informed.

H.J. Tidy
contact@n*******.com
Re: Re: Re: Re: Strange experience – mine
5 Messages
Nicole.Rain <nicrain@********.com> December 14 2019
To: contact@n*******.com
H.J. Tidy,

It's not over.

The night after I sent you the last email, I had a very frightening dream. I was standing at the end of a dark hallway. I don't know where the hallway was. It seemed to go on forever. I felt like I was waiting for someone, but it wasn't someone I wanted to meet. You know that feeling when you are about to be punished for something and you can't escape. You're just waiting for it. That's what I felt.

Then this girl appeared. She didn't walk down the hallway or anything. She was just there. She was a little girl, maybe six or seven, in a red skirt and with a bob haircut. She had black hair and very white skin.

Her voice was not a child's voice. It was deep and booming. She said, "I've been trying to talk to you. I want to drag you to hell."

Then she smiled, such a sweet, girlish smile, and reached for me. I pulled my arm away, but where her fingers touched me, it hurt.

I woke up then, but my arm still hurt. I have burning scratch marks on my arm, just like I saw on my door.

I've been getting more texts and even emails, all telling me about horrible things that will happen to me.

What's worse, I swear I see her sometimes. Just out the corner of my eye, I see this little girl staring at me. If I try to look at her directly, I can't see her, but I know she's there.

I swear she's here now, while I type this to you. She scares me. I think she knows what I'm saying to you.

Help me, please. I don't know if I'm going crazy or what. I'm scared. Maybe crazy would be better. Better than what I think she has in mind.

Please, H.J. Tidy, if you can suggest anything – help me.

Nicole
nicrain@********.com
Re: Re: Re: Re: Re: Strange experience – mine
6 Messages
H.J. Tidy <contact@n*******.com> December 16 2019
To: nicrain@********.com
Hello Nicole,

I'm sorry it's taken me so long to reply. This time of year can be a bit chaotic.

What you've been telling me is a bit worrying. I talked to a friend who has some experience with demonology, and he made some suggestions about what the name that you started to get might be. I won't tell you what it is. I don't want to write it down. But it worries me. I would like you to seek some help. Talk to a priest. Get the police to keep a better eye on your place, or maybe move out. Go stay with some friends for a while. And get rid of that phone. Replace it.

Please keep in contact and let me know how you are getting on. I might be able to get you some more advice soon.

H.J. Tidy

nicrain@********.com
Re: Re: Re; Re: Re: Re: Strange experience – mine
6 Messages
H.J. Tidy <contact@n*******.com> December 18 2019
To: nicrain@********.com
Hello Nicole,

Have you had a chance to take any of the steps I suggested? I'd like to know if you've had a chance to get rid of the phone and stay with some friends. I think that would actually help you. Let me know please.

H.J. Tidy
nicrain@********.com
Re: Re: Re: Re; Re: Re: Re: Strange experience – mine
7 Messages
H.J. Tidy <contact@n*******.com> December 23 2019
To: nicrain@********.com
Hello Nicole,

I haven't heard from you. Please let me know you are okay. I worry about you. Steffi says she hasn't seen you for days.
H.J. Tidy
We haven't heard back from Nicole after this. I don't have much information about Nicole besides her email address. I hope she's alright and whatever was bothering her was taken care of.

Chapter 4
Dad's Painting

The house was silent, absolutely silent. Then a scream broke the silence, but I was alone in the house.

I guess it started when Dad bought the painting. Now my dad isn't an art expert, but he does love a bargain. He found a painting on eBay, an original piece, that no one seemed to be bidding on. Dad snapped it up, virtually sight unseen. He spent days crowing about his "great buy."

When it was delivered, a few days later, the first surprise was the size. Apparently, Dad hadn't checked that out. It was 24 by 36 inches, so not small. Mom was not happy, but Dad said he'd move some stuff around in the living room, and there'd be space for it.

While Dad had been talking, all I'd been able to see was the back of the painting. When he turned it around, I felt uneasy. The picture was of a young boy, about five, with short black hair, standing in front of a glass-paneled door, with a female doll propped up beside him. On the other side of the door, pressed up against the glass panels, were hands, many hands. The whole image made me uncomfortable. The boy was frowning, looking unhappy, and almost aggressive. The doll had no eyes, just black holes. And the hands, well they were quite disturbing, at least to me.

Dad, however, was still thrilled. He kept going on about how lucky he was to get such a great piece, which apparently represented the line between fantasy and reality or something. He propped it up on an ottoman in the living room, saying he'd get around to mounting it on the wall "one day." We'd all heard this from Dad before. "One day" could very well be no day.

After dinner that evening, I happened to look at the painting again. The boy's eyes struck me. The more I looked at them, the more they seemed to suck me in. I stared. It was almost as if I was looking in a mirror. His eyes and my eyes felt connected. He blinked! I saw movement. My heart leaped into my throat. I wanted out. I wanted to back away, but I seemed rooted to the spot. I couldn't move. The eyes never left mine.

"What ya doing?"

My sister's voice broke the silence and seemed to knife through the connection between me and the painting. I turned away and was overcome by a sudden feeling of dizziness. I dropped into a chair, careful to avoid any glance at the painting.

My sister came up to me. "You okay? You look terrible."

"Yeah ... I ... just dizzy."

I shook my head. I'd been up since early that morning, and I'd been out all day in the sun. Must just be a touch of sunstroke or something. I grabbed a bottle of water and headed off to bed.

As most people would, I rationalized that experience. I just assumed it was me, my mind playing tricks on me. I'll admit, though, that I always tried to avoid looking at the painting when I went into the living room. Even without that strange moment, the picture would have still creeped me out. It just had that weird vibe to it.

It took me a while to realize it, but my sister was avoiding the picture too. Now, I have to admit we didn't talk that much. She's four years younger than me, which, given I was 15, was enough to make our relationship rocky at times. It's that family thing, being too similar and too different at the same time.

Anyway, I noticed that she would always choose a seat that kept the painting out of her immediate sightline whenever she was in the living room. If she had to go across the living room, she'd always try to stay as far away as possible, even if that meant going well out of her way.

Usually, if I'd noticed behavior like that, I'd have used it against her, teased her about it. That's what older brothers are supposed to do. Not this time, though. This time I shared at least a little of her fear.

One night, when our parents had gone out, we were sitting in the dining room, and I asked her about it.

She replied immediately and seriously. "The boy is evil," she said. "The whole picture is evil. I don't like it."

I didn't laugh. Instead I asked, "Why do you think that?"

She leaned across the table and looked me straight in the eye. "The thing it rests on, the ottoman, it moves," she whispered.

I was going to laugh, tell her to stop trying to tease me when I saw the look on her face. She was serious, deadly serious. And she was scared.

"When?" I asked.

"When Mom and Dad aren't in the room. Suppose no one's looking straight at it. It moves. It shakes. It's scary."

I felt I had to do the big brother thing, be the voice of reason. "It could just be vibration. You know, if a truck goes past outside."

She was silent for a few seconds. I could see a conflicted look on her face. I thought she was trying to process what I'd suggested. She wasn't.

"It's in my dreams," she whispered.

"What?"

"I dreamed. I was walking through the house. I came down the hall. The door to the living room was closed, but a red light was coming all around it. I was going to open the door. Then, from nowhere, there was an angel standing there. He was tall, blond, with big white wings and a sword of fire. He stopped me and said, 'Do not enter the living room. Never at night.'"

"Well, that's just a dream." I was trying to do the big brother thing again.

"That's not all." There were tears in her eyes now, and she looked scared. "I've seen the boy."

"The boy in the picture?"

"Yes! I was sleeping. I felt something pull on my leg. It pulled stronger and stronger, shaking me. When I opened my eyes, I saw the boy—from the picture—he was there, grabbing my ankle. I couldn't move. I was so scared."

"And then?"

"I'm not sure. He turned his head like something got his attention. Then he disappeared, and I was lying in my bed."

She was crying now. I tried to convince her it was all a bad dream, nothing more, but I was not convinced myself. I sat with her in her bedroom as she went to sleep that night, only coming out when Mom and Dad came home. I'm not sure if I stayed with her because she was scared or because I was.

A couple of nights later, I was home alone. The others had gone out to a birthday party for one of my sister's friends. Because my parents knew the friend's parents, they'd gone together. I had no interest in an eleven-year-old's birthday, so I stayed home.

I was in my room, surfing the net. I felt uneasy. My desk faces the window, so I sit with my back toward the door to my room. Every few seconds, I'd get that feeling that someone was out in the hall, looking in at me. I'd turn, and of course, there'd be no one there. I was alone in the house. I couldn't shake that feeling, though. At the time, I thought it was guilt. There are certain websites that a 15-year-old looks at only when he's alone in the house.

I couldn't even concentrate on my surfing. I shut down the browser and looked behind me again. No one there! I realized that the house was silent. That seemed a little strange. Any house has some noise, and we lived on a reasonably busy road. I couldn't hear a thing. It was like something had muffled the whole world. It was uncanny. I concentrated, trying to hear anything.

Then a scream split the silence. My whole body leaped out of the chair. It was a scream of absolute horror and fear. It sounded like the scream of a young boy, and it came from inside the house. It sounded like it came from my parent's room. But I was alone in the house, and I knew that.

The silence again. The same silence. The same absolute silence. My heart was still racing. My hands were shaking. I tried to get a grip on myself. It was just an illusion. Someone outside screaming, though I knew I'd heard the sound from inside the house. Maybe I'd fallen asleep in my chair for a second. I dreamed it all!

Then I realized the house was no longer silent. I could hear the music. A child singing? It was quiet at first, but it started to build. My phone, maybe. Maybe it'd switched to some dumb ringtone or something. I picked it up. The screen was black. I pushed the button, still black. The music was getting louder. It was not coming from the phone. Nothing was coming from the phone. It was dead.

I jumped out of my chair and dove across the hall into the bathroom. I slammed the door shut and quickly slid the lock. The bathroom is the only room in the house with a locking door. I huddled in a corner, on the floor, my eyes on the locked door, as the music rose louder and louder.

Then it stopped. Nothing. Silence again. Total silence.

I was frozen in the bathroom. There was no way I was going out into that silence. No way was I going to see what was happening out there now.

I started to relax a little when I began to hear loud noises again. The silence had gone. I stayed in the bathroom, though, till I heard the sound of my parent's car pulling up the driveway. Then I slipped out of the bathroom and back into my room, to bed, though it took me a long time to get to sleep.

The next day was sunny and clear. In the daylight, in the sunshine, all my fear of the night before faded away again. I told myself it was nothing. It must have been a dream or something. It couldn't have been real.

As it got dark, though, my unease returned. There was a feeling in the house. It wasn't just me that felt it. We all seemed upset, easily annoyed, jumpy. My parents had a huge argument, something they rarely do. My father slammed the door of their room, and my mother said she'd sleep on a sofa in the living room. My sister, desperate for company when she slept, said she'd sleep on the other couch too, to "keep Mom company."

I went to bed, feeling that the whole house seemed to be smothered in a haze of darkness—nothing physical, but a suffocating feeling that seemed to have spread across all of us.

Surprisingly, given my feelings and what had happened the night before, I fell asleep almost instantly. Later I dreamed.

I was standing in the hall, just outside my room. It was our house, but it was "wrong." All the windows were black like there was nothing outside the house. Like you do in a dream, I somehow knew something was coming. I turned toward the stairs. The lights on the stairway were on, but they started to flicker, slowly at first, then faster, almost as quickly as a strobe light.

I walked toward the stairs and looked down. In the flickering light, I saw a small figure walking up toward me. I could barely make out his appearance. He seemed to be a young boy, but the colors were all wrong. His skin was gray, his clothes black. His head was down so that I couldn't see his face.

Suddenly, the lights went off completely. I was left, petrified, standing in the darkness. Then they came back on.

The child was standing right in front of me at the top of the stairs. I knew he was small, but somehow he also seemed my height. I could look him straight in his face. His gray features were contorted into a look of hate and aggression. He hated me! I could see it. His eyes glowed yellow and seemed to be getting brighter, burning into my mind.

My thoughts rushed back to barely believed religious instruction. "In the name of Jesus, leave me alone!" I shouted at him.

He vanished. I was left standing alone at the top of the stairs.

Then I woke up. My room was pitch dark. My heart was pounding, and I was drenched in a cold sweat. I didn't want to move. I didn't want to do anything that might draw attention to myself. The dream had felt so real, so true.

Finally, I gathered my courage and reached for my phone to check the time. 3:00. I'd have to find a way to get back to sleep.

Then a scream ripped through the night. This time I recognized the voice. It was my sister.

I leaped out of bed and raced downstairs to the living room, arriving at the same time as my father. We both rushed into the room to find my sister and my mother huddled together on the sofa, their faces white, their eyes staring.

My father rushed to comfort Mom, all thoughts of their argument gone. I hugged my sister, feeling her galloping heart through her pajamas.

"What happened?" Dad asked.

"Not here," Mom replied.

At my mother's insistence, we all moved into the dining room. With hot cocoa and coffee made, my sister told her story.

She'd been asleep on the sofa. Something had grabbed her ankle and started pulling. She'd had an old blanket pulled over her face, but it had a hole in it, and she'd seen who was there.

It had been a little boy, about five, with short black hair. His face, though, seemed to be falling off his skull. She said she could see bone poking through. His eyes were empty black holes.

She'd closed her eyes, not wanting to see any more. Then it seemed to stop, and she felt like she woke up again. The boy was standing in the living room. He started to run, faster than any little boy could, out the living room door, back in again. Then he stopped and stared at her. She said the stare felt evil, like she could feel the hate flowing off him.

Then she screamed, and he vanished.

My mother had been quiet through this story. She looked concerned, though. I asked her why.

"Your sister's screaming woke me up. It gave me quite a shock," she said. "Just as I was opening my eyes, just as I was waking up, I could have sworn there was another person in the living room with us. I didn't see him clearly, but just for a second, I'm sure I saw someone small standing there."

All three of us turned to Dad.

"Get rid of that painting!" Mom said. My sister and I nodded.

Dad, to his credit, didn't argue. The very next morning, he took it in his car. On the way to work, he dumped it behind the old brewery. He said no one would ever find it there.

I hope not. I don't want anyone else to go through what we did.

Chapter 5
Lady in White

It was right there beside me. I could see all the details, but somehow, I couldn't see the face. I'm pretty sure I didn't want to see the face.

It was a family vacation I would never forget. Usually, when you say that, you're thinking about the great times you had. What's the worst thing that happens on a family vacation? Maybe you get in an argument with an aunt or something. Not this time! This one was way beyond anything like that. This one was the most frightening thing I've ever experienced.

I was twenty-eight at the time and between jobs. That's a different way of saying I was unemployed. It's not as bad as it sounds. I'd lost my old job when the company went bust, but I'd already had several employers expressing interest. I suppose you could say I was making the most of a temporary and unexpected vacation.

I was staying with my parents in Tampa. I'd been in New York for four years, and this was a great time to reconnect before I went off somewhere else. It was made even better when Dad came home and told us all he'd received a very generous bonus on his latest contract. To celebrate, we were going to do something he'd always want to do. Take off for the weekend for a vacation in the Dominican Republic.

Don't ask me why that was on Dad's bucket list. I have no idea, but I would not turn down a free vacation in the Caribbean. A couple of Dad's colleagues were going to come along as well. Apparently, Dad wasn't the only one to do well out of the contract.

The next Saturday, bright and early, the five of us flew into Santo Domingo. Along with Dad and his friends were Mom and me. We were all looking forward to a great weekend.

We hired two cars at the airport and then drove over the island to the hotel. Dad had booked at Las Terrenas. It was beautiful and very comfortable, but Dad didn't plan on staying there. He planned to use the hotel as a base and maybe stay there if the weather turned bad. What Dad really wanted to do was spend a night in the open air on a beach a bit further east up the coast that a friend of his in Las Terrenas had told him about. Like I said, for Dad, this was a bucket list trip.

We had lunch and then stocked up on essentials, beer mostly, before driving east. The scenery up there was beautiful. And the beach, well, it was exactly what Dad said it would be. At the end of a rough dirt track was an incredible broad sandy beach between the low hills and the Atlantic. There was no one else on the whole length of it. We had the entire thing to ourselves.

We had a fantastic afternoon. The water was just right for swimming. There were crabs and fish, all easy to catch. The breeze kept the temperature cool enough to be comfortable, but not cold. It was idyllic, and if that was all that happened, it would undoubtedly have been a vacation to remember.

At some point, I noticed that the sun was getting pretty close to the hills to the west. That seemed like a good time to get some wood and get a fire going on the beach. One of Dad's friends, Dane, wanted to cut some branches off a tree, but I pointed out that there was more than enough dry drift-wood above the tideline, so we got that instead.

By the time the sun vanished behind the hills, we had a pretty good fire going. Then it was time to get the fish and crabs cooked and the beers opened. There's nothing like an open fire barbecue on a tropical beach with some good, cold beers. I felt like I could stay there forever, like it was heaven.

By about nine that night, we were all well-fed and happy. Dad was particularly delighted; he'd had most of the beers. I wasn't a big drinker back then. I'd only had a couple. The beach, the fresh seafood, and the amazing tropical night sky were enough for me.

I don't know who first heard the noise. It started very quietly and slowly built in volume. Soon we all had that slightly concerned look on our faces, where you know something's not quite right, but you don't know what it is. Conversations around the fire fell off.

"What's that?" Mom asked, the first to break the silence.

It seemed to be wailing, like a woman in pain or in the most profound state of anguish. I pushed that thought out of my head. We hadn't seen another soul since we got to the beach.

"An animal?" I suggested. The faces around the fire didn't look convinced, but they covered it with nods and grunts.

An animal, we seemed to tacitly agree, even as the wailing rose and fell irregularly around us. The conversation resumed, but it had a forced quality. The laughs unnaturally loud, the pauses too long, and filled too abruptly. I guessed I wasn't the only one feeling a bit nervous, but I pretended not to be, just like everyone else.

The wailing had died again when Dad said, "Who's that?"

We all turned to see what he was looking at. About a hundred feet away was a figure, waist-deep in the sea, apparently walking toward the beach. At first glance, I was baffled. It seemed to be a strange white half-human shape. Then, in the light of the fire, I made out the form better. It was a woman with long black hair that hung almost to her knees. She was wearing a simple white dress, wet and clinging to her body. When I'd first seen her, the black of her hair had blended seamlessly with the night sky, confusing me.

She walked out of the sea, up the beach, looking straight ahead.

Dane called to her. "Hey! Hey, you okay?"

She seemed not to hear him. She kept on walking through the sand and disappeared among the trees at the edge of the beach.

There was silence at the fire for a minute. Then everyone started talking at once. A local. Obviously. Been swimming? In that dress? Collecting crabs? Maybe she doesn't speak English? Yeah, must be.

Mom, who had also refrained from drinking much, nudged me in the ribs. "Daniel, go see if she's okay."

I got up. I didn't really want to go looking for the woman. I didn't know if any of the others had noticed it, but I had. There was something strange about the way she walked. In the dim light, I couldn't identify it, but I knew I'd seen something odd. However, Mom's orders are not to be disobeyed.

I had a rough idea of where the woman had gone into the trees. I walked a little way in among them myself, but I couldn't find a path. There was, as far as I could tell, nothing there. No path, no woman, and no light or house that she could have gone to. I did spot a couple of footprints in the soft ground by the trees, but they seemed to be leading to the sea, not from it, so I disregarded them.

When I came back to the fire and reported my findings, nothing, the conversation died again. Dane seemed about to say something when there was another sound. Not a wail, more of a whirring, flapping. Then we saw silhouettes against the stars and realized what it was. Birds! Lots of birds flying away from the forest.

"Odd," noted Dad. "What scared them away?"

That really did kill the mood. Everyone now seemed to be straining to hear what might be in the forest. I know I was. I could make out the gentle lap of the sea, the slight rustling of the trees in the breeze, but nothing else. Aren't tropical forests supposed to be noisy? Where were the insect noises, the bird calls? The hair on my arms started to rise. This situation was getting creepy. I turned my head, staring at the trees. I could have sworn something was staring back at me, but I couldn't see anything. I felt cold. I knew the night was still warm, and the fire still blazed, but I was no longer warm. I was shivering.

Something hit the beach. There was a thud, the sound of something heavy landing in the sand. It seemed to be about fifteen or twenty feet away from us. We all jumped. The noise had seemed so loud in the silence.

I went over to where I'd heard the sound. Nothing! The sand was undisturbed. Dad made some comment about me being blind and came over to look. He couldn't see anything either. Everyone got up, looking around the beach, near the fire. I think we just started looking because it felt better to be doing something instead of just sitting there, waiting. Waiting for what we couldn't have told you.

Mom said what I was wondering. "Should we go back to the hotel? Maybe staying out here isn't the best idea."

Dad snorted. Nothing, as far as he was concerned, was going to drive him away from his night on the beach.

We stood around, looking at each other. I know I wanted to leave. I was thoroughly spooked. I didn't feel comfortable on that beach at all.

I opened my mouth to tell Dad, but a scream cut me off. It was a woman's voice, piercing and unbelievably loud. She sounded as if she was in absolute agony. Worse, it didn't stop, but just kept on going for at least a minute. There was never a pause for a breath.

Then the scream halted. It didn't wind down or anything. It just stopped. In the silence, I could hear the sound of foot-steps running up the beach. It sounded like someone run-ning from the sea to the trees. I spun to look, but the beach was clear. It didn't stay empty for long. A coconut flew out of the night sky and buried itself in the sand near my feet. Then more came, flying out from the trees and landing on the beach.

Dad was silent, but his face was clear enough. I've never seen my father look so scared before, and I hope to never see it again. He said nothing, just put down his beer can and started packing up his stuff by the fire.

Somehow, as if his example had broken the spell, we all started doing the same. We jammed things in bags. We pulled clothes back on over our swimwear. No one spoke. We were all hurrying to pack.

Then the screams started again, rising and falling this time. Dane gave up packing, grabbed his stuff in a big bundle, and started running for the cars. The rest of us followed. Getting off the beach seemed much more important than maybe losing some sunglasses.

Dane and Dad's other friend reached the cars first. They jumped in one and were gone even as we reached the other. I threw my stuff in and jumped in front. Mom and Dad quickly got in the back. I fired up the car and aimed for the path off the beach.

We'd just got moving when I noticed a figure standing in the mouth of the path. I hit the brakes. In the light of the headlights, I could see a woman, in a white dress, with long black hair. It was the same figure we'd seen emerge from the ocean. I couldn't make out her face. It was hidden behind a curtain of black hair. I did notice her feet, though, and I felt a shiver rush through me. Her feet were backward. It looked like her knees went the wrong way. There was such a feeling of wrongness just looking at her I felt almost ill. I certainly didn't want to drive any closer, but I didn't want to stay on the beach either.

The car shook. There was a bang. Something had hit us from behind. Instinctively we all looked behind us, but there was nothing there.

I turned forward again. The woman had gone from the path. We could go!

I heard my mother gasp. Something made me look to the left. There she was. Right beside my door. She was so close I see the damp cotton of her dress. It seemed that I could see her with unnatural clarity. I could make out the brown stains at the end of her fingernails. I could see the fine hairs on her arms. I couldn't, for some reason, make out her face, though.

The black hair hung lankly in front of it, moving slightly, but behind the hair, I could see nothing.

I screamed and floored the gas. The car leaped and stalled. She was still there. I fumbled for the key, trying not to look out my window.

The engine caught, and we sped away. I didn't look in the mirror. I didn't want to see what was behind us. I just concentrated on the track ahead of us and drove as fast as I dared.

We hit the main road at El Limon. I could feel my shoulders relax as we raced past actual lights again, but Dad had no intention of stopping. This place was too close to the beach.

By the time we hit the outskirts of Las Terrenas, we had all started to relax a bit. There was even a bit of conversation in the car, mostly questions about what we had seen. Questions none of us could answer.

The car shuddered to a halt about eight hundred yards from our hotel. Instantly I started looking for the woman in white again, but we were in town, and there was no strange woman. It seemed we'd just broken down.

Dad was going to go to the hotel and ring his friend, but Mom stopped him. Like me, she was worried about him. He'd had a lot to drink and a lot of scares. He still looked paler than I can ever remember seeing. Instead, Mom took the number and headed for the hotel herself. I stayed to look after the car and Dad.

I'm pretty sure Dad was in shock. He kept asking questions and jumping between topics. Why had Dane not waited for us? What was that thing? Why hadn't his friend mentioned her?

Danilo, Dad's friend, arrived in a pickup truck not too much later. He towed us to the hotel and then came in for coffee.

We told Danilo what had happened, and he turned pale, looking at us in shock.

"You should not have been there at night," he said. "I told you about the beach because it is beautiful and unspoiled, but if you had told me you wanted to stay at night, I would never have let you. Bad things have happened on that beach at night. People have walked into the sea, almost as if following someone, to never be seen again. Many people have been injured there at night. Only last week, a pregnant woman went there at night. Her child was stillborn the next day."

"What was that thing," Mom asked. "It looked human, but its hair, its legs ..."

"It is called la Ciguapa. Some say she's a demon. Others say she is a Nature guardian. If you harm her forest, she will punish you. All I know is, you are all lucky to have come back here in one piece."

I leaned back in my chair and let out a sigh. Nature guardian? What would have happened to us if I had let Dane cut that tree? I decided I didn't want to know.

Chapter 6
Grandma's Doll

My clothes exploded out of the dresser. They hung in the air for a minute. Then the door opened. My Grandma stood there ... "We finish this now."

All this happened when I was just a little girl, but I remember it well. It was the weirdest thing that's ever happened to me. I don't know if I should be writing it down, though. People who hear this story have told me weird stuff happens to them after they listen to it. It's like, somehow, the thing knows when it's being spoken about, and it makes itself felt.

I want to write this down, but you don't have to read it. It might find out you've read this. If something happens, it's not my fault, okay? Ah, the hell with it. Read it. I don't care.

So, I was a little girl, eleven. That summer vacation, I went to stay with my Grandma in Key West. I know what you're thinking: old folks in Florida, what a cliché. Well, it's a cliché because it's true. When my Grandpa died, my Grandma left North Dakota and moved to Florida. The money from sell-ing the farm bought her a good-sized house on Eaton St. She loved it—the weather, the people, the lack of winter.

My mom decided a couple of years after Grandma had moved south that I should go and spend two weeks of the summer vacation in Florida. My mother said it was so I could spend some "quality time" with my Grandmother. Right. She just wanted me out of the house for two weeks, and, honestly, who could blame her. Kids can be okay, but they can also be a considerable drag. It didn't hurt that I loved my Grandma back then.

Grandma's place was big, huge to an eleven-year-old who'd lived her life in a trailer park in Billings. It was an old Victorian house, with two floors and a turret-type thing poking out the top. I called it a turret. Grandma called it the attic. Grandma was what you might call practical-minded.

I had a room, a huge room that led onto a balcony, all to myself. I was in eleven-year-old heaven. This was all so different from Billings. Of course, if Grandma had given us some of the money from the farm, instead of buying a giant retirement house, we wouldn't have been living in a trailer.

The morning after I arrived, Grandma showed me around. I have to admit, it was a beautiful house, all old with high ceilings and lots of rooms. Why Grandma needed such an extravagant place all to herself, I'll never know.

Finally, we went up the little staircase to the attic. It wasn't an attic in the sense of a dark and stuffy room. It was the turret of the house, with lots of windows. It felt just like another room, but it was dusty and musty. A mix of older people smells and dust. Grandma kept a lot of old junk up there, including stuff she'd found in the house when she moved in. She might have been practical-minded, but she was also a bit of a pack rat.

Of course, to an eleven-year-old, all that junk was just a massive pile of treasure. I seem to remember having a great afternoon, just looking through stacks of stuff with Grandma. Amazing what a child finds interesting.

Among all the junk was a doll. It was old and handmade, but to young me, it looked quite cute. It was just a cloth doll, about half my height, yet somehow it seemed to me to be a great toy. My Grandma disagreed. When I showed it to her, she frowned. She said something about it being "too old and dirty" and then, as adults do, distracted me with some other nonsense.

When we came down from the attic, Grandma locked the door. She told me some nonsense about the attic having some dangerous stuff in it and made me promise never to go up there alone. Well, the rest of the house was huge. I had no problem agreeing to that.

The next morning, as I came down the hallway, I noticed that the attic door was open. I didn't think anything about it until Grandma blamed me for it. She got all angry and accused me—me!—of going up to the attic in the night. Said she'd heard movement up there around one in the morning and found little footprints in the dust. Well, back then, I was a good little girl. I was fast asleep at one, dreaming, oddly enough, of the doll. Besides, I didn't have the key.

I finally managed to make her believe me. Once she did, a strange look crossed her face, and then she was all smiles again and talking about what we'd be doing that day. Old folks and their dementia.

On the second morning, the same thing. The door was open. This time, Grandma didn't try to blame me. She just did that frowning thing and closed it up again before we went out for the day to meet some of her friends and their grandkids. That's Florida in summer for you, old folks, and their grandkids.

When we got back that afternoon, there was a surprise in my room. There was the doll from the attic sitting on my bed. I guessed Grandma had slipped it into my room some-time before we left. I heard her going up to shut the attic door again, in fact, as I picked up the doll. I hugged it to my chest and was going to go running off to thank Grandma. Somehow, though, the thought popped into my head that I shouldn't. Somehow this was just for me, and Grandma didn't need to be thanked.

I held the doll at arm's length and stared at it. Its little black eyes seemed to stare back at me. As I looked at them, I got the feeling that I didn't need to thank anyone. The doll would look out for me. The doll was my friend. Well, what girl doesn't want a friendly doll?

At dinner that night, I seemed different. Nothing Grandma said seemed to make me happy. We got into an argument, and I got sent to bed early. Well, I had my new friend. I slept with the doll.

In the morning, we both tried to forget what had hap-pened the night before. Grandma said I was obviously over-excited and tired. I let it go, but really, what would an older woman like her know about a child's feelings?

In the afternoon, Grandma went out and left me in the house. She said I needed some rest, and to be honest, I was a bit sleepy. I lay down on the sofa for a nap. The sun com-ing in the window and the peaceful surroundings made for a comforting and relaxing environment. Soon I was in that half-asleep, dozy state.

I heard the den door open and the sound of footsteps on the wooden floor. I was so relaxed I just waved a hand and muttered a quick, "hi." Then the footsteps went back to the door, and I heard it open.

That was strange. Grandma would always reply when I greeted her. I sat up, opening my eyes, just in time to see the door swing shut.

Worried somewhat that Grandma was somehow still mad with me, I got up and went to her room. She'd always change when she got home. I knocked. No response. I tried it again. Nothing! Alarmed—what if she'd died or something?—I entered, but no Grandma! The room was empty.

I started checking the house, trying to find her. Then I thought, what if it's a thief? I ran to my room. I was relieved to see that the doll was still there, though he was on the floor, not on the bed where I'd left him. Well, he must have fallen off.

I was still there, hugging my doll, when I heard Grandma come home thirty minutes later. I decided not to tell her about the noises. I had probably just dreamed it, and you know how old folks get about things like that. She'd likely call the cops or something.

Hearing footsteps, though, is something people tell me happens after they hear my story. It's like they hear, or read, the doll's story, and then they hear something in the house with them, especially if they are alone at night.

I don't want you to think I spent the whole time in Florida with my Grandma. I didn't. There were other exiled kids sent to their grandparents for the summer. I got along okay with some, though my best friend in Key West was Tyra Fox. She was from Louisiana, and her family was loaded. Don't think that's why I wanted her as a friend. It was only part of it. She was also a really down-to-earth girl.

Tyra came around one afternoon. We went up to my room, and excitedly she showed me what her parents had given her. She had a brand new digital camera. Those things weren't cheap back then. She was freaking out about it, as girls do, you know. Then she saw the doll.

Tyra wanted to get a picture of the doll, but I wasn't so sure. I felt—I don't know—like it didn't want its photo taken. Tyra brushed that off. She lined up and took a shot of the doll on my bed. When we looked at the picture, it was a bit weird. The only part of the doll in focus was its eyes, and they were red from the flash. The rest was blurry like it had been moving. Tyra liked the picture, though. She said it looked "creepy." Oddly, I can't remember Tyra using the flash.

I saw Tyra the next day. She was pale and worried. "I had to delete that picture of the doll," she said.

I asked her why.

"I put it up on my computer. When I brought it up, the lights started to turn on and off in my room. I thought there was a problem with the house's electricity. My dad went down to the basement to check the electric board. He said it was open, and some of the breakers, including the one for my room, were tripped. But my computer never went off."

I nodded, but I thought she was being a bit silly.

"Then," she continued, "my cat came in. She jumped on my lap and looked toward the computer. She changed at once. She hissed and growled at the computer, then she swiped at me and ran off. Look, I've still got claw marks on my arm. I deleted the picture, and nothing else happened."

I saw the cuts on her arm, but I said she was just acting silly. The doll was lovely, and it loved me. It was mine. It made me feel good.

Since then, I have heard of similar experiences from other people. Animals were behaving strangely at just the mention of the doll. Lights were flickering. Maybe it has some truth.

"It's evil," said Tyra.

Well, that was enough. Silly stories are one thing. Insulting my doll was another. I threw her out of the house and never saw her again. Grandma asked what was wrong. I just said Tyra was "stupid."

Grandma looked at me funny and said she was going to tidy my room. That was fine. Saved me doing it. It was only after she'd been gone for ten minutes that I remembered the doll.

I ran up the stairs, but Grandma already had the doll and was heading for the attic. I cried, I begged, I shouted at her. Nothing would stop her as she took it back into the attic. When she came back down, I told her I hated her.

She pushed me down into a chair and sat next to me. She started talking, even though I was still crying. She started going on about how I'd changed. When I'd come to her, I'd been "nice," according to Grandma. Then I'd met the doll, and I'd become different. That's what she said. I was eleven, so I believed her. I stopped crying. I hugged my Grandma and promised I'd never go back into the attic for the doll. Strangely, I actually meant it.

We got all dressed up and went out to dinner at a fancy restaurant that night. I was impressed. I felt all grown up in my dress, dining on fine china. I have no idea how much Grandma paid for that meal, but looking back, I figure it was probably more than we'd spend a week on food in Billings.

I felt like a little princess when I got back to Grandma's. I slipped into bed and drifted off into dreams of princes and unicorns, the silly stuff of an eleven-year-old's fantasy.

I woke up hearing my door close. I guessed Grandma had come in to check on me. It gave me a warm feeling.

Then I heard another noise. It sounded like one of my drawers opening and then closing. Couldn't be. In the faint light of my room at night, it was clear there was no one there.

Then the closet door opened. I heard it, and I saw it, dimly, move. It stayed open for a minute, then slammed shut with a bang. I was going to scream, but fear kept me silent.

Then my dresser started to move. First, it just seemed to shuffle a little. Then it moved properly, sliding forward, toward my bed. I couldn't believe it. My eyes were focused on it, trying to see in the dim light who could be moving it.

The dresser got closer to the bed. It didn't look like it was going to stop. It was going to hit the bed with me in it. Suddenly my frozen body started to move. I pushed myself to the other side of the bed, and I screamed. I let out all the fear and panic I had in a long and loud scream.

As I screamed, the drawers on my dresser sprang open. All of my clothes exploded out of the drawers and hung motionless in the air over my bed.

Then the door opened, and the light came on. The clothes all dropped onto my bed, and I saw Grandma standing in the doorway, looking at the foot of my bed.

There, sitting on the footboard, was the doll. It seemed to be looking straight at me. I hadn't brought it in here, and Grandma certainly wouldn't.

I leaped out of bed, into Grandma's arms, shaking and crying. Her face was a mask of hate. It wasn't directed at me, though, and she was staring at the doll.

"We finish this now," she said in a voice I'd never heard from her before.

Grandma made me put a coat on over my pajamas, and then we got into the car. The doll went into the trunk. In the middle of the night, we drove down to the end of Duval St.

Grandma made me stay in the car. Then she went to the trunk and got the doll. With a strength I didn't think she had, she threw the doll out into the sea.

We went back to Grandma's place, and the next week passed peacefully. Boring is what I'd call it now. I felt more like myself. Grandma and I never fought. She was very kind and generous to me, and I felt very thankful to her.

There was one odd thing. The day I left, Grandma gave me the key and sent me to the attic to get a photo album to take home for my mother. I found it quickly enough and started to head for the attic door.

Then I got a bad feeling, like someone was in the attic with me, staring at me. I turned around slowly, and there it was. The doll was sitting on top of a box by the window, all dusty, looking just like it had when I first saw it. Part of me wanted to grab it and take it back to Billings with me. I started toward it when Grandma called up to me from the bottom of the stairs. At the sound of her voice, I suddenly had the opposite feelings, like I hated and feared the doll. I ran for the door and down the stairs.

After I got back to Billings, my mother said she'd never send me to Grandma's again. She said I came back "bitter" and "nasty." I think I came back smarter and less childish.

I've seen the doll sometimes, on the internet or TV. Every time I see it, I realize I should have taken it with me that day.

Chapter 7
Shack in the Woods

I was awake. I knew that. I couldn't see anything, certainly nothing of the noise that had woken me. But I could feel very strongly that I should not be there.

It was not a dark and stormy night. It was a slightly overcast morning and humid. In the summer of 2007, I lived in Virginia, not far from Lexington, in a little town on the James. My place was right at the edge of town, backed up to the woods. It was perfect for those weekend morning walks.

I was out on my Saturday morning walk, but there are not many people up there. There are pretty clear paths through the woods near the town. I was strolling, somewhat aimlessly, down one of my favorite tracks when I saw movement ahead. I rarely saw anyone when I was out in the woods, so I was a bit surprised. I strained through the slightly misty forest air, trying to make out the figure.

Then the mist parted briefly, and I saw a familiar brown jacket and camouflage ball cap in the sunlight. It had to be

Larry, the guy who had the place next to mine. He was a great, friendly guy, though I'd never seen him out in anything except that jacket and hat. A creature of habit, I guess.

Larry was terrific, but that yapping little dog of his was a pain. The damn animal would be up, barking, at all sorts of hours. It didn't seem to bother Larry, but it bothered me. Come to think of it, though, I hadn't heard the dog last night.

I quickened my pace slightly, aiming to catch up with Larry. He was always good for a chat and a laugh. No matter how hard I tried, however, I didn't seem able to shorten the distance between us. Frustrated, thinking he may have seen me and not felt like company, I finally slowed and looked around me.

I was in a part of the woods I'd never been to before. That didn't worry me; I have a pretty good sense of direction, and I knew all I had to do was go downhill to get back to the path. I was surprised by the woods, though. I was sure I hadn't gone significantly far, but here the woods were much more overgrown than the area I usually walked in. There were brambles and extensive undergrowth under the trees, though the plants had a brown and sickly look. The trees themselves seemed stunted compared to those closer to the river. It reminded me of the forest I had once seen south of Khabarovsk, in Russia, where industrial runoff had polluted the ground. There was no industry up in these hills, though.

As my mind was processing this, my eyes drifted along the treetops. There. Smoke. Not much, but a slight trail of gray slowly climbing into the clearing sky. So, something was going on up here.

Curiosity got the better of me. I hunted around the trees and the brambles, looking for a path to the smoke. Eventually, I found it, rough and slightly overgrown, but definitely winding away toward the smoke. I pushed through the tangled growth and followed it.

It came out into a small clearing among the stunted trees. At the far side, backed up against the trees, was a building. To call it a shack would be generous. It seemed to have been thrown together from bits and pieces of other houses. It was wood, mostly, with boards laid horizontally, but with an apparent disregard for color or size. There were spaces for windows but covered in rotting plywood. A stone step led to a doorway with no sign of a door. The roof was metal. At least three different shades of paint peeked through the rust. At the top, on the far side, was a crooked chimney made from an assortment of bricks and stones. A thin plume of smoke rose—or more correctly, leaked out of it. I'd found the source of the smoke.

I started across the clearing. I'd found the place now, and I had a strong desire to see what was going on in there. I paused, though. The hills around here could be home to any number of less than friendly folks. They could be growing drugs, hunting illegally, or any other activity that meant they wouldn't welcome visitors. Of course, if that were the case, they'd probably already seen me. I decided to be friendly and hope things would pan out okay.

"Hello!" I shouted. "Anyone there?"

There was no response. In fact, there was no noise. The whole forest seemed to have frozen. I couldn't hear a bird, a cicada, or even the breeze in the trees. It was as if a cone of silence had fallen over the whole clearing.

I felt that there was something, or someone, around, though. The hairs on the back of my neck were up. I felt nervous and jittery. A part of me wanted to be out of there. I was still curious, though. I was also a little worried that someone might be in there and just waiting for me to turn around before, what …? I wasn't sure, but I felt I should try to communicate again.

"Is-" I cleared the sudden blockage in my throat and tried again. "Is anyone there?"

The silence continued. The world seemed shut out of that little clearing. I felt like I was standing on an alien planet. I shivered. Logically, I should have just backed out of the clearing and gone home. I guess I wasn't that smart. There was smoke coming from the chimney. Someone must be there, someone who didn't answer me. Maybe someone who couldn't. Perhaps someone in trouble was injured. I figured I should have a quick look in to make sure no one needed help. Or perhaps I just gave in to my curiosity.

I looked in the doorway. The sky was still overcast, and there was no light in the cabin. I couldn't see a thing. I took a couple of steps inside, moving to one side to let the weak daylight in.

As the light trickled in, I could barely make out along the back wall what looked like three people. No, three vats, or flasks. Each quite large, brass maybe, and connected by …? Tubular piping. Brass pipes. I let out a quick laugh. Moonshine! It was a moonshine still. Couldn't stand the stuff myself, but if that's what folks were up to out here, good luck to them.

I took another couple of steps inside, admiring the pipework when the smell hit me. Now I've smelled stills before. They're not unpleasant if kept clean, but this smell was different. It was a putrid sickly-sweet smell. It made me gag at the back of my throat. I shook my head to clear it.

That's when I saw the pile beside the still. At first, I thought it was just a pile of rags or something similar, like you often find in places like this. But rags don't have fur or legs. I took one step closer, over the rickety boards, trying not to gag anymore on the odor.

Crap! It was a pile of animal pieces. What the hell were people doing up here? Fur, skin, bones, legs—I stopped looking and stepped back.

My foot hit something as I retreated. I waved my hands, briefly fighting for balance before I crashed to the floor. My head hit something hard. I saw stars, real stars. My vision spent a few seconds coming and going, and that was before the pain of the impact managed to work its way into my consciousness.

I groaned. I shook my head and tried to get my bearings again. By my head was a large and quite solid-looking brick. Well, that explained the pain.

Then I looked down at my legs. There was a metal bucket by my left foot. It was obviously full, as it was heavy enough to trip me, but not fall over itself. I rolled over and pulled myself along the floor to look at the offending bucket. I didn't feel up to standing just yet.

One sight, and smell, of the bucket and I just about threw up. Floating in a mix of blood and other bodily fluids were pieces of rotten meat, browns, blues, and different colors, I didn't want to see. I pulled my head back and lay on the floor again, fighting down my rapidly rising bile. My head was still swimming, and the contents of the bucket had not helped. I felt terrible, but everything I'd seen made me want to get out of that place. I steeled myself to rise.

Something grabbed my ankle. I looked down. That bang on my head must have done a lot of damage. I saw, somewhat unclearly, a hand. The skin was white, almost as white as chalk, but each finger ended in a long, black, pointed nail.

I looked up further. The hand was attached to an arm, covered in a rotting cotton sleeve. I still felt dizzy, but I could make out the vague shape of a man in the darkest corner of the cabin. His hand was on my ankle, gripping it tight.

"Let go!" I shouted. "What are you doing?"

The man made no response, but he started to pull. My head was still swimming, but this made no sense. I'm muscled, a good 200 pounds, but this skinny arm was slowly dragging me across the floor. I grabbed at the boards, trying to slow my movement.

The clouds outside broke briefly, and sunlight flooded into the cabin. I wished it hadn't. Whatever was pulling me looked even less human. It was tall, way too tall, and thin. Its arms seemed twice as long as they should be. Its legs looked far too thin to hold up its bloated body. Its head was still in shadow, and I felt unreasonably thankful for that.

I scrabbled at the floor, even more desperately, as it slowly pulled me ever closer. My hand found the brick and closed over it. Frantic and almost beyond thinking, I hurled it toward the monstrous creature.

I heard the impact, a sickening soft sound. Then it screamed. It wasn't a human scream. It was a high, piercing keening that cut straight to my bones.

The hand dropped off my ankle, and I staggered to my feet. I had no more curiosity. I wanted out.

I lurched across the floor, rebounding off the door frame, and out into the blessed sunshine.

Shaking my head, trying to clear the fuzziness in there, I jogged for the path. Behind me, I heard movement, the creak of floorboards. God, was that thing coming after me?

I picked up my speed, driving through the underbrush and out to the main path. I sprinted, or tried to, my balance wasn't so good, down the trail. I could hear a thumping sound behind me. I had to get away, get down the path, get back to town.

I can't remember much of that run. I fell more than once, but I never wanted to look behind me. When I reached the bottom of the hill, I was exhausted. I could run no more. I could still hear a thumping. It took me a moment to realize it was the blood pumping in my head.

Unable to run any more, I slowly turned my head to look behind me. The path was clear. The birds were singing above me, and the clouds had cleared. I managed a smile. I took a step. The world spun around me, and I collapsed into oblivion.

The policeman listened intently to my story in the hospital. The nurses had told him I was concussed and suffering multiple minor injuries. I guess he didn't know whether to take me seriously or not.

By the time I was well enough to be discharged, I seemed to have him convinced. Both of the local cops accompanied me up the hill the day after I left the hospital. I hadn't accurately described where the cabin was, but I could take them to it. I do have a pretty good sense of direction.

We found it quickly enough, though on that day, there was no smoke from the chimney, and the birds were out in force in the clearing.

I refused to go inside. There are some things you just can't do.

When the cops came back out, their faces looked a lot paler. They'd found what I'd said. They identified the remains of a deer, a mountain lion, and Larry's dog. There were other animals remains, but they were too far gone to identify. All the identifiable animals had had their blood drained.

There were a few mysteries left. Whoever had been in the cabin had left no evidence of their identity. A camera left nearby showed no one entering the cabin for the next six months. After that, they tore it down and buried the remnants.

No one could identify the material in the still. It was undoubtedly not moonshine, but no one could work out what it was and what it was for.

Oh, and Larry said he'd never been out that morning. So what was I following? Was it leading me up to that cabin?

I didn't wait for six months. I have no idea who or what was in that cabin. I think I don't want to know. What it was going to do to me—I have even less desire ever to find out.

I left that little town a week after the event. Now I have an apartment in inner-city Chicago. People tell me it's not safe, but I like it. There are no trees.

Chapter 8
Tell Me Your Name

I found this in Travis' room. I don't know what he was writing it for, maybe just for himself, but I doubt that. We worked together, Travis and me, for the National Park Service. I'm not going to tell you which park. That might be a bit too much information, not that it matters, really. You won't believe me, but I got no desire for someone to come out here and start bugging me about all this.

On the other hand, Travis wrote pretty well. I reckon his work should see the light of day. I figure no one will believe it anyway, but maybe it is the right thing to do. Perhaps some of you will listen and take a bit more care in the woods when camping. Perhaps it will lift a little weight off my conscience.

This is what he wrote:

September 3, 2020

Yesterday I had the weirdest experience of an already odd year. I mean, sure, 2020 is one for the history books, and we still got three months to go, but this was just the oddest thing I've ever heard. I yet don't know what to make of it, but I think I should write it down. I want to remember this.

I've been out here for six months now. I did all the training and got posted to a small park back in March. It was great to have a job and a career when other people I know weren't doing well.

I got partnered up with Sam. She's great, knows her stuff, but she won't put up with any foolishness. Not just that, she could kick my ass from here to Canada and not break a sweat. She's a tough thing, but I'd trust her with my life.

At this point, the Park is getting pretty busy. With all the COVID restrictions, people can't travel overseas anymore, so they seem to be coming out here more. Of course, that does mean more people drinking and doing foolish things. Your average city visitor is not really at home in the wild. Which means more search and rescue for people like Sam and me.

Today was another one. Sam and I were called to a campsite just outside the woods. A couple in their twenties had wandered off and not returned. By the time we got there, it was 4 pm, and they'd been gone since 12, so it wasn't just a matter of a young couple looking for a private spot for some serious "bonding." No, these people were definitely lost.

Sam was not very happy about this. She seems to have a pretty low opinion of people who only leave their cities once a year. We have a job to do, though, so we started through the woods, heading in the direction they gave us.

Sam's not a big talker, so things were pretty quiet as we headed in among the trees. As I started across a small clearing, I saw movement out the corner of my eye. I caught a quick glimpse of a woman, maybe ten yards away. It seemed like she had brown hair, perhaps, and blue clothes. Despite the distance, I could hear a weak voice calling, "Help me, please."

I started to turn toward her, and suddenly Sam was in my face. Her hands roughly grabbed my head and stopped it from turning.

"You don't want to do that," she said. She grabbed my shoulder and pulled me forward, away from the woman.

"But, there's a girl," I said, trying to turn my head.

Sam got to one side of me, between the girl and me. "I know, kid," she said. "Just keep walking forward."

She pushed me hard, sending me stumbling forward while she shouted at the forest. "What's your name?"

The woman, whoever she was, didn't answer. All I could hear was, "Help me, please. I really need help." Her voice seemed to be getting weaker.

Sam was behind me now and still pushing me away. She shouted again. "Tell me your name, and we'll help you."

I heard the woman's voice again. "Please ... I need help so bad. Travis ... please."

I stopped still until Sam shoved me in the back again, sending me forward. The woman had called my name.

I took a couple of steps and swung back to face Sam. "She said my name. She knows me. We have to help her. It's our job, dammit!"

Sam stepped right up to me, her face inches from mine. Her face had a strange mix of anger and fear. She stared straight into my eyes.

"You wanna go, you go alone," she said. "And if you do, you ain't coming back. I'm not going to vanish just 'cause you wanna play the hero. Now get moving, and come with me."

She pushed past me and kept heading out of the clearing. I wanted to see who the woman was. I wanted to help her, but something in Sam's face made me think again. Numbly, feeling guilty, I followed her out of the clearing.

Not long after, we found the missing couple. I was barely listening while Sam berated them. They sheepishly followed us back to their friends, and then we went back to the station.

As soon as the door was shut, I asked, "What was that about?"

Sam flopped into a seat. "What? Dumb townies don't know if they get lost going uphill. They should go downhill?"

My feelings from the afternoon boiled over. She'd been bossing me around like I'd failed a test, like there was something I should know and didn't.

"No! That woman. Why'd you push me away?"

She didn't look at me. "Long story."

I refused to be put off. "I've got time. Spill."

Sam sighed. "You really want to know? Okay. I'll tell, but you got to promise me you're not going to tell anyone."

"What is it?" I asked. "Some sort of hazing for the newbie?"

She looked up at me, not a trace of humor on her face. "Promise, kid."

I sat down and looked at her. Her body language, her face, all spoke of a resigned misery. She didn't look like someone who'd just hazed the new kid. She looked like someone with the weight of the world on her shoulders.

"I promise."

At the time, I meant it. Now, I don't know. Maybe people need to know.

The story Sam told me went something like this:

"Honestly, I don't know what they are. I don't think anyone does. My old superior didn't know, and he'd been here for forty years.

"The first day I was here, he tells me, you hear a girl calling for help in the woods, don't go help her. Don't look at her. Don't do anything unless she can tell you her name. Why? 'Cause those things don't have names. Maybe they don't understand what a name is. Perhaps they don't understand the question. Perhaps they figure they're so powerful they don't need one.

"Thing is, though, they'll do anything to make you look at them. They'll call for help. They'll be all pathetic like, pleading with you. A young guy like you, they might be offering sex. They'll say they know you, know your mom, anything to get you to look at them."

I wasn't really following this, but I asked, "What happens if you look at them?"

"I had the same question. Adam, my old boss, he didn't know either. He does now, but he isn't around to tell. See, all I know is if you look at them, you walk off, and you don't come back."

This was getting weird, so I thought I'd shift the subject, maybe get a second opinion. "Where's Adam now?"

She laughed, more of an abrupt snort. "He looked."

Sam wasn't looking at me anymore. She was staring out the window, focused on nothing I could see, but I guessed she was reliving everything she told me.

"It was a stupid lost dog. Some idiot lost their dog up past the West Ridge. We were out looking for it, Adam and me. Then from behind us, we hear a voice calling 'Adam.'

"Now that didn't work. We keep moving forward. Then we hear a girl's voice, a panicked girl's voice, the voice of a scared child. 'Grandpa,' it says.

"Adam's granddaughter, she'd died, drowned in a pool about four months before. That voice, though, it sounds just like her. I see Adam come to a halt. I see him turn around. I hear him whisper, 'Aubree?'

"I can see the exact moment he looks right at it. His eyes got huge. Then they glaze. His face just goes slack. He starts walking, walking back to where the voice was coming from.

"I scream at him. I shout, but he just walks past me, heading back behind me, to the voice. I want to turn, to stop him, but there's no way in hell I'm looking back there. He passes me, and I start walking the other way, away from the voice. I'm not going back there. I walk away like a coward. And we never found his body."

Sam stopped for a minute and then turned to me, focusing on me again.

"We never found his body," she repeated. "You never do find any bodies. We found his old Army dog tags and his wedding ring on a branch halfway up a tree. I got no idea what happened to him or the others, but I know he never returned. I never want to find out why."

She got up and grabbed a beer from the fridge. She finished the can faster than I'd seen her drink before.

My head was swimming. I didn't want to believe her, but the way she'd spoken, the certainty in her voice, and the apparent dismay over her cowardice convinced me. Then I felt a chill. If she was telling the truth, then those things were out there. I'd nearly looked at one today. Then another thought struck me.

"Why don't other people know about this? Why isn't something being done?"

Sam shrugged. "People know, some people. And, in the end, rather them than us."

"What are you talking about?"

"Look, Travis, understand this. It, or they, I don't even know if it's one or more, but whatever, it needs people. So we close the park. Then what? Do you think it'll stay here? Nah, it'll go hunting. You want that Thing in the suburbs, or you want it here taking the odd idiot?"

I was shocked by her callousness. I wanted to argue, but something in her face told me this was not the time.

That's what happened yesterday. I wrote it down as well as I can remember it. I don't honestly know what to make of it. I can see that Sam believes she is telling the truth. I know what we heard in the forest yesterday. It's all so unreal, though. That's why I want to write this down. I want to be able to come back and look at this later and see what I should do after I've had time to think.

September 15, 2020

It happened again. Now I really do believe Sam.

Some unprepared tourist had gone and broken his ankle in a ditch. Sam and I went out to get him.

As we walked toward the site of the accident, I spotted movement out of the corner of my eye. I guessed what it was. Even worse, we would have to walk past to get to the site. I felt my flesh crawl. Sam's story suddenly seemed too real. I did not want to get close to whatever it was.

In a panic, I stopped Sam and asked, "What do we do now?"

Sam said, in what I thought was an amazingly calm voice, "We walk on. Getting close doesn't cause any problems. Don't look, and you'll be fine."

We kept walking down the path. I found myself getting closer to Sam than normal. I guess I just wanted that human companionship.

"Help me, please help me," the voice started. This time it was a child's voice.

Sam kept looking straight ahead. I didn't have the strength, and I looked down at the ground. I heard Sam ask its name.

It didn't give a name. Instead, it said, in its childish voice, "Please. I'm so hungry. I think I'm lost. Help me, please."

We kept walking on, getting closer. It was hard to ignore its childish, begging voice.

"Travis. Sam. Someone ... please help me ... I'm so cold."

It took all my self-control not to look up. We got a few yards away, walking past the spot where the voice was coming from. It kept whining at us.

"Please ... you have to help me ... please."

As we passed, I felt it. A wave of cold seemed to flow over me as if I'd just opened the door to my freezer. Goosebumps ran up my arms. My teeth chattered.

I could smell it. It smelled like dirty pond water, like a pond that had no outlet and had started to go bad. The smell was piercing. It seemed to climb into my nose and up into my brain.

I felt wrong. My body told me that this was a bad thing. There was a feeling in the pit of my stomach, like that feeling of anxiety just before something terrible happens. And you know you can't stop that bad thing. At that point, I knew Sam hadn't lied to me. That Thing was real, and it was wrong.

As we passed, it called after us. "Where are you going? Come back. I need you. I want my mommy."

As we got further away, it seemed to stop. I don't know if we just got so far away we couldn't hear it or if it gave up. I know I never want to get that close again. I never want to feel like that again.

October 16, 2020

I've started looking into these things. Certainly not looking at them. Since I've been here, over a hundred people have gone missing. Over a hundred. Not that you'd know it. The local cops know what the situation is. They provide convenient documents for us to sign: accident, animal attack, drowning. It's all covered up.

The Thing, or things, has gotten over one hundred people in this park. What if it's not alone? What if others are hanging around in other parks, other wilderness locations? How many more people do they get?

I can't stay silent. I need to let people know. If I say nothing, I am complicit in their disappearance, or worse. I have to get a message out. I'm going to post this journal, maybe with a couple of the police reports.

If you are in a park, be careful. If a girl calls you, don't look at her, not until she gives you her name. I don't know what happens if they do get you, but I know you never come back. Be careful, please.

October 18, 2020

Before I post this, I need to get some more evidence. I think I have an idea about these things. I've been doing some research.

I think they are related to the Sirens of Greek mythology. If that's true, they don't tell us their names because, in mythology, names have power. If I can find their names, then I can control one, bring it to the public. At that point, I'll have all the evidence I need to convince the world that these things are real. It's a risk, but it's worth trying.

That's the end of Travis' story. You can believe it or not. I'd like to say I don't care, but that's not true. I know the truth. I know there's something out here, and maybe, if you know too, you'll be a bit more careful. Possibly there'll be one or two less missing people out there. Perhaps I'll sleep better knowing I've done something.

Travis won't be bothered about me posting his story. I guess he tried his experiment. We currently cannot find Travis. He vanished two weeks ago. I honestly don't think we're going to find him.

Chapter 9
The Neighbor

It was growing! Its human skin dropping off. There was nothing I could do. I was frozen with fear.

I met Joseph in Durango, Colorado about twenty years ago. I was in my usual spot in the diner just off East 8th when this guy comes in and sits down at the counter next to me. He was dressed like a farmer, all dusty and sweaty, but his eyes were different. They had a haunted look, the thousand-yard stare I used to see in guys coming back from the jungle over there.

The waitress, Ruby, came over, and this guy stammered that he wants a coffee, strong and black. Nothing unusual in that, but the way his hands moved, flitting around like a couple of nervous birds, the way his eyes tried to be everywhere at once, that got my attention. The guy was young, maybe early twenties. Didn't look like a vet, but he was acting like he'd just escaped from the worst firefight in history. I couldn't help myself. I hate to see people suffer, and I swung around to face him.

"You okay, son? You're looking pretty strung-out."

He spun on his stool and looked at me. I swear it took him a good five seconds to actually focus on my face and really see me. His eyes kept drifting away.

"I'm good ... tired ... just tired," he said.

I smiled my best emphatic smile. "Son, I see a lot of folks come through here, a lot of them tired. You're well beyond tired. What happened?"

He finally looked me in the eyes. "You wouldn't believe me."

I widened my smile slightly and waved Ruby over for more coffee. "Try me."

He looked around him like someone was going to jump him. Then he looked back at me. "Hell, I gotta tell someone, but I promise you are not going to believe me."

This is the story Joseph told me, minus the pauses, the prompting, and most of his more colorful language.

So, I work, or I guess I worked, on a farm down in New Mexico. I'm not telling you exactly where, but in McKinley County. I had a little house on the edge of the property. I did my work, got paid, and didn't see many other people on most days. It was a good life, comfortable, and with an income that was pretty decent for the area.

Most days, after I'd done everything that needed doing, I'd go for a walk in the evening. Out there, on a good night, it's beautiful. You couldn't count all the stars in the sky. The ridge, silhouetted against the starry sky, was beautiful. I loved my evening walks, just me and the stars. You feel like you're the only person in the world, and it's all yours.

One evening, a couple of nights back, I stepped out for a walk. It was still cool, even though it's June. Probably in the mid-40s, but that never worried me. The cool air makes you feel alive.

It was still light, and I hadn't gone far, up toward the ridge, when I spotted a blood trail on the ground. Not much, just a drop here and there. Still, you learn to spot things like that when you live out there. I figured it was a deer, injured by a coyote or something, and followed it.

When I lost the light, I lost the trail. There are lots of stars in the sky up there. But following a blood trail at night, even with starlight, is beyond me. I'd come a fair way from the house and started thinking I should probably head back. But, I felt restless, like I had to go somewhere, do something. Nothing I could put my finger on, but just a feeling that now was not the time to head back. I didn't have much to do the next day, so I just let the feeling guide me. I kept walking, assuming that at some point I'd get tired, the restless feeling would run out, and then I could head home.

It must have been about midnight when I hit the road. Now, calling it a road is a bit generous. It's a dirt service road, but it's the best we've got for thirty or forty miles, so it's "The Road."

I stood there for a minute, idly kicking the stones up the road and staring at the sky. Then I got "the creeps." You know that feeling like you know someone's watching you? I felt like there were a pair of eyes burning into my back. You live alone, in an area that's got wild animals in it, you learn to trust feelings like that. I turned slowly to look along the road. No wolf or mountain lion was standing there, just a man.

Not many people will be walking around out there at midnight, and I recognized this one straight off. The heavy sheepskin vest and the wide-brimmed hat all meant it could only be George Sullivan. He worked on the next farm over. It might be a few miles between us, but it was about as close to neighbors as you get in that sort of place.

Seeing me looking in his direction, George waved and came over. This was a bit strange. George and I were nodding acquaintances, not really friends. Nothing wrong with George. He just liked his own company.

"Hi Joe," he said when he got close. "You're out late tonight."

"Yeah," I responded. "Felt a bit restless. Needed to stretch my legs, I guess."

"Me too." It sounded like he was smiling, but it being night and him wearing the wide-brimmed hat, I couldn't tell. "Feel like I might head up to the ridge. Want to come along?"

Now that was just weird. George never usually sought out company like that. It was the middle of the night, and I started to feel that something here just wasn't adding up. I didn't feel restless anymore. I just wanted to get back home.

"Nah," I said. "I think I'll head back."

"Fair enough. I might as well keep you company to the fence line."

That made sense, the fence line would give him a straight run up to the ridge, but it just didn't sound like George's usual behavior. There was a little voice somewhere in the back of my head whispering that something was off. I couldn't exactly tell him not to come with me, though, so I turned and headed back.

George fell in step beside me, and we started back toward my place. That's when I gagged. Something, somewhere, stunk. It was a sweetly putrid smell, the worst thing I've ever smelled in my life. Somehow it seemed to combine rotting meat, rotting fruit, and rotten eggs. All rolled into one. It brought a tear to my eyes.

I turned to George. "God, what's that smell?"

He paused and seemed to sniff the air for a second. "I guess something's died out there." He turned his head to me. "Happens now and again."

I was going to say more, but something stopped me. Instead, I walked back toward my house with George at my side. I know we talked on the way back, but I can't for the life of me remember what we talked about. It's like I was on autopilot, responding without thinking, till we got to the fence line.

There, George wished me a good night and headed up for the ridge. I went straight back to my house. Thankfully, somewhere around the fence line, the smell seemed to disappear. I'd had enough that night. I kicked off my boots and crashed on top of my bed.

That night I had an odd dream. I was talking to Mike Hannett, another one of my neighbors. Behind him was a churchyard, the one at Saint Patrick's in Vanderwagen. There was a funeral going on. Mike kept trying to explain something to me, but I could never make out what he was talking about. He was very excited and acting as if he needed me to understand something, but I just couldn't make it out. I awoke, thinking there was something there I needed to grasp. Whatever he was talking about was important, but the feeling faded as I started on my day's jobs.

I had some shopping to do in Gallup that day. By the time I got back, it was mid-afternoon. I flicked on the TV as I came in. It provided background noise while I put stuff away in the kitchen. Just as I came back out into the living room, something was on about a missing man being found dead. The reporter said something was odd about the case, and I turned to pay a bit more attention. Just then, the TV seemed to lose the signal. The screen dissolved into static. Well, it probably wasn't important anyway.

I had an early dinner that night. Then the restless feeling came over me again. I hadn't planned to go out for a walk that night. George had spooked me the night before, but somehow I couldn't stop myself. Anything I tried to do in the house just seemed like a waste of time. The magazine I'd been reading was meaningless, and the housework I'd planned on seemed like a waste of time. Realizing I couldn't fight it, I pulled on a jacket and headed out. This time, though, and unlike my usual practice, I took along a large flashlight.

There's nothing like a good walk to clear your head. As I made my way, without thinking, toward the dirt road that runs along the base of the ridge, my subconscious was putting the puzzle together. The dream. Mike. The funeral. The blood trail. The missing man. George.

George! I'd reached the road without really noticing. There was George, standing there, almost as if waiting for me.

"Out late again, Joe?" This time I really could hear the smile. "How about taking that walk tonight?"

He stepped toward me, and again I smelled that awful odor of decay. I took a step back, gagging. I'd been expecting the smell, but it was still overpowering. I'd worked it out. This was not George. Three days ago, Mike had told me about the funeral he'd gone to. George's funeral.

I backpedaled a little more down the road. George, or whatever that was, followed. "Where are you going, Joe?"

I brought the flashlight up and switched it on, shining it into the thing's face. It was George's face, in a way. The cheeks and the tip of the nose had already started to decay. The eye sockets were empty, but there was a red glow behind them. The lips, cracked and weeping, were twisted up into a smile.

It was not a friendly smile. It was the smile of something who had just seen its next victim, the slightly ironic grin that suggested it was enjoying itself at my expense.

I was stunned, frozen in place. I felt like a rabbit in a car's headlights. As I stood, transfixed, the smile broadened. The grin stretched and finally ripped the face of my old neighbor. The lower half of the face fell away, and I could see a mouth filled with far too many teeth that now stretched in a grin from ear to ear.

I felt myself getting smaller. No, that wasn't right. It was getting taller. It seemed to slough off the human skin, like a snake shedding. As the covering fell away, I saw its legs, gray, spindly, and lengthening. Now it stood a good foot taller than me.

Something dragged my screaming mind back to reality. Something clicked in my brain. I turned and ran! I leaped from the road, up onto a path into the woods at the base of the ridge. The sanest part of me hoped to lose whatever it was among the trees.

My flashlight was dying. I switched it off and shoved it into my jacket pocket. The action distracted me, and I stumbled over a root. Barely recovering my footing, I glanced back over my shoulder.

I hadn't lost it. It was stalking along behind me. It no longer made any attempt to look human. In the dim starlight, I made out a tall gray body. It must have been eight foot tall, but spindly and thin. It was almost a giant walking skeleton, covered in gray skin. It was all out of proportion, though. Its legs were ridiculously long, its arms ended in curved talons somewhere near its knees. I didn't stare long enough to make out the face, but I saw two glowing red spots where the eyes should be and a black maw for a mouth.

I'd seen enough. I put on another burst of speed, adrenaline giving my legs strength I didn't know they had. I risked a quick glance back. I noticed the thing was barely jogging. It was toying with me. It could catch me any time it wanted to. There was no chance I could outrun this thing. I had no hope.

I reached an especially dense part of the wood. I was out of the thing's sight for a few seconds. There was a slight chance if I could move quickly. I grabbed a branch and hauled myself up into a tree, climbing as quickly as I could until I would be above its eye level.

I had barely stopped climbing when it came around the trees below me. I kept my hand over my mouth, trying to calm my panting, desperate to make no noise.

It halted. Its head swung around on its spindly neck as it checked out the area. It seemed confused to have lost me. Then it wailed. I've never heard any sound like that before. Its scream sounded like a crying baby who'd been badly hurt, but mixed into that was a more profound, angrier noise. I can't describe it any better than that. I also can't explain how it was able to make that scream for what seemed like a minute, without taking a breath.

The noise was enough to cover any I might make, though. While it screamed below me, I unscrewed the flashlight as quietly as I was able and slid a battery out. When it stopped screaming, I hurled the battery as far as I could into the woods.

The battery struck a tree. The thing's head snapped to that direction, and then it was off, racing through the woods faster than I thought possible.

As soon as it left, I climbed down the tree as quickly as I could and started running down the trail, back to the road.

I reached the road and stood for a second, panting. Then the sound reached my ears. It was a sound I'd heard before. There are deer up in the forest along the ridge. Now they were coming my way. I tried to get out of the way and just managed as they broke from the wood cover. It looked like the whole herd, rushing out of the trees and along the road. They ignored me, their eyes rolling with fear.

Too late, I realized what they were running from. The gray figure bounded out of the woods, standing there, not five feet from me. This was it then.

One of its taloned arms flashed down. It smacked into one of the deer, sending it sprawling. Before the deer could right itself, the gray creature twisted its body, its mouth gripping the deer's neck. There was a crunch of bone, a splash of blood, and the deer stopped moving.

I backed slowly off the road. I don't know if it was the dust the deer raised, the distraction of the deer themselves, or the fact it was already eating. Whatever the reason, I was able to slip away. I crept back into the field, and when I felt safe enough, I ran.

I got back to my house and piled everything I could into my truck. Then I left. I've been driving ever since. This is the first time I've stopped. I'm going to have coffee, some food. Then I'm leaving. I'm going north, as far as I can. There is no way I'm staying anywhere near here.

That was Joseph's story. Despite what he said, I believed him. I'd heard enough of Skinwalkers before. He was a fortunate young man to have escaped this one.

I gave him some advice, including the address of a Navajo friend he might like to talk to before he left town. I doubted he would, though. He seemed determined not to stop south of the Canadian border.

Once I finished my coffee, I left the diner and started driving south. He may not have told me exactly where all this happened, but he'd given me enough clues. In the middle of the afternoon, I turned up a country service road that ran along the base of a wooded ridge. As I came around a corner, I startled a small herd of deer. They scattered, diving for the trees.

All except one. It stood there, watching me drive past. I swear it smiled.

Chapter 10

Classified

Editor's note: The following was found on a laptop recovered in 2016 from a crashed car approximately seven miles northwest of Rachel, Nevada. The deceased driver's identity has never been established, and the vehicle's registration proved to be a fake. Files on the laptop were extensively encrypted, and it required several years before some could be decrypted. The following is one of the more interesting files recovered. We offer no suggestions regarding the provenance of the material. It is provided simply because we feel it may interest the reader. Readers may draw their own conclusions.

TOP SECRET – UMBRA
141445ZS JUNE 2008 STAFF
CITE DCD/------------------------
TO PRIORITY DCD/HEADQUARTERS
ATTN: ------------------------------
FROM: DCD/----------------------
SUBJECT: CASE ------------------ UFO CONTACT
REF: (a) DCD/HEADQUARTERS 14596

(b) SUBJECT REPORT DATED 9 JUNE 2008, UFO CONTACT STUDY

1. SOURCES FULL NAME IS ---------------------------
--. HE IS EMPLOYED AS -------------------------------------
-- AR

2. REFERENT b MATERIAL CLASSIFIED TOP SECRET/UMBRA AT REPORTING AGENT'S DISCRETION. REQUEST FURTHER ADVICE AND FOLLOW UP INSTRUCTIONS FOR POSSIBLE --------
----

REFERENCE b
AGENT RESPONSIBLE ---------------------------------

1. The following material is a transcript of (subj identified in point 1 above) description of his encounter with non-human entities of an unknown type and his analysis of the importance of the interaction. Conclusion and recommendations follow at the end of the transcript.

2. NOTE – transcript has been edited for readability due to subj confusion and disorientation following the acquisition. Some material has been paraphrased to improve readability. All references to the interrogator and enhanced interrogation methods have been removed.

TRANSCRIPT FOLLOWS

Look, I've told you guys, weird things happen around me. I have no control over that. I don't know what more you want from me.

Okay, okay. Yeah, I've got an idea what's been causing all this. You called them visitors? That's as good a name as any, I guess. Yes, I've met them.

My first meeting? It's hard to tell. Even early in my life, I had some strange dreams. Some of my earliest memories are a bit strange. I met people no one else met. I saw things in the sky, but no one else seemed to notice them. But the first encounter I can recall clearly would have been when I was around six.

Yes—six! You said the earliest, well, that's it.

We were living with my Nana at the time. We? We being me, my mom, and my brother. You guys seem to know everything. You figure out what happened to my father.

So, we were living at Nana's. My brother and Nana's rooms were upstairs. My mom's room and my room were in the basement. It was comfortable, but I admit my Nana always seemed to treat me a bit oddly, a bit differently. Like she could see something different in me. I think she put me in the basement to keep me away from her.

Yeah, so I'm all tucked up for the night. It was a chilly evening, and I had my Scooby-Doo comforter on the bed. All snug like a six-year-old should be. I drifted off to children's dreams. Though, even back then, I had some pretty odd dreams.

The next thing I know, I'm suddenly awake, just like someone turning on a light. Usually, I'd take a bit of time to wake up, but this time it was instant.

The first thing I think is, I'm cold. I'm freezing. I was warm in bed, and now I'm not. I figure my comforter's fallen off or something. I reach out to grab it, or at least I try.

I can't move. My arms, my legs, nothing. No matter how I try, they just don't move. Now I'm getting scared.

My eyes snap open. I can see I'm not in bed, not even in Nana's house. Now I'm terrified. I do what any six-year-old would do. I scream. 'Cept I can't. My mouth won't move. I can't make any noise. I struggle to, and nothing happens. That freaks me. I'm six. If there's a problem, you scream, and people come and help you. Now I can't do that. There's no help coming. I'm terrified.

I can see a bit around me. It's not my bedroom. The whole room is white. There's light, real bright, but I can't see where it's coming from. It just seems to be all around the room, like the whole room's equally light.

Now I'm sure I'm not in my bedroom. I'm certainly not in my bed. I feel like I'm on a cold, flat, metal table. That's the best way I can describe it, like I'm a slab of meat in a butcher's window.

Now, the light's blinding, and I can't move my head, but I can see some movement. There are others in that room with me. I can't make them out clearly, but they aren't human. I can see that.

They're tall, tall and really skinny. They got big heads on the end of real spindly necks. I don't know how they can hold their heads up on those necks. I can't see faces. All I can see are silhouettes against the light of the room. They're just dark shapes moving around the sides of my vision. They're not moving like people. It's like their legs bend in two different places as they walk. My mind goes through a whole list of possibilities, trying to identify them but gives up in the end.

A six-year-old doesn't have a big enough frame of reference. I'm not sure an adult does, either.

My mom said I got a gift. I can feel people, you know, like positive and negative energies. Well, these folks didn't have any. I mean, I was happy that I wasn't picking up any negative energy, but there was no positive as well. It was almost like they weren't actually there. I mean, they're moving around like they were alive, but I look at them and wonder if they really are.

They must have realized I was awake about that point. They start telling me they aren't going to hurt me.

No, not talking. There's no language. That's the thing. The whole time I was there, I didn't hear a single thing. There was absolutely no noise in the room. A place like this one we're in has a fan, and noise like that all the time. That had nothing, absolutely nothing. Even when these things were walking around, there was no noise. No footsteps. It's like what people say. The silence was deafening.

Instead, I heard them in my head. It wasn't words, more like a feeling, an idea. I got this feeling from them. They wouldn't hurt me, and everything would work out fine. I felt it, I believed it, I stopped trying to scream. I relaxed.

There's about four or five of the things in there. While they're sending me those peaceful ideas, they start getting closer. I should have been scared. Thinking back on it now, being six, I should have been terrified. I wasn't, though. I trusted them, I trusted them so much, and I just relaxed.

The next thing I know, it's morning. I'm in bed. All tucked up again. I do notice Scooby-Doo is upside down. I try to sit up, but I get real dizzy. I lie down again and give it a minute, then I try again, and I'm fine.

I am all confused. It's like, to me, that the room was the most real thing and that my bedroom is somehow less real. It takes me the better part of the morning to see things the other way around, to understand that the world is not a dream.

Yeah, I try to tell Mom, but, come on, I'm six. However, I try to explain it, it comes out garbled. Mom says something about dreams or imagination. I know it was no dream. I can still feel their thoughts, the reassurance, in my head. Somehow, I don't want to tell Nana.

It's ten years before I tell anyone else. My friend and I were out back of his place, smoking some weed—yes, that's in my file—and I tell him the story. He's like, "Man, you got abducted by aliens."

The weird thing, I'd never even thought of that before. It's like I'd always been directed away from that idea. I'd always laughed at things like that on the TV. I never even watched science fiction, though I loved hearing about space. Now, though, it seemed to make sense.

What? Purpose? Yeah, I got an idea about that too.

I was talking to my cousin a little while back. She's big on many of these ideas, probably done a lot more reading than I have. She said I could be a Starseed.

You guys got to read more if you're going to do this job. A Starseed is an advanced spiritual being from another realm with advanced spiritual and or scientific knowledge from thousands of years ago.

In particular, she said I might be a Lightworker. Before you ask, a Lightworker is a unique soul who chooses to incarnate on Earth to raise the spirituality and consciousness of all those around them. Wouldn't that be cool? I'm here to help raise everyone's spiritual level to something better.

So, yeah, I figure that explains why weird stuff happens around me and why I do the things I do.

What do you mean I have to stay here longer? Come on. You can't keep me here forever. People are going to notice. Who are you guys, anyway?

END TRANSCRIPT

ADDITIONAL OBSERVATIONS

1. Attempts to corroborate subj's story by contacting family members have drawn a blank. His mother is in a state mental facility and has been unresponsive for the last fifteen years. Attempts to locate subj's maternal grandmother have failed. She seems to have vanished shortly before his sixteenth birthday. There is no evidence subj ever had a brother.

2. There are inconsistencies in subj's birth documents. These are minor, but there is some evidence that much of the subj's documentary material was created or modified around the time he was six years old.

3. Much of the subj's recall matches similar individuals interrogated by this facility or agents thereof.

4. Subj's associates have reported various "weird" events associated with him and unusual behavior. Again, these match similar individuals.

CONCLUSIONS—EYES ONLY

1. Given the subj's recall and the additional evidence cited in OBSERVATIONS above, it is possible that the subj is not entirely who he believes himself to be.

2. The subj's claim to be a STARSEED may have some validity. It is possible that he is acting under the influence of forces neither he nor we understand.

3. Despite the subj's belief that these forces intend him to act for some "better good," we have no evidence that is the case. The subject may be under the influence of a species whose moral judgment is different from our own. I refer the reader to the subj's observations regarding the apparent lack of positive or negative "energy" in his abductors. There is no reason to believe that their goals match ours or even the human race's.

4. Despite the standard procedure, it is true that the subj cannot remain here for any length of time. His absence from public view would soon be noticed.

5. Subj must be forcibly reminded of national security requirements before resuming his normal existence. Warnings regarding the sanctions available if security is breached must be made clear to the subj.

6. Under no circumstances should the subj be allowed to win elections to any public office or continue to hold any authority position. All means necessary to achieve this should be considered.

7. Given the risks involved, no further human agents should be used in this case. We should use only our agents.

Chapter 11
Lonely Cabin

I was awake. I knew that. I couldn't see anything, certainly nothing of the noise that had woken me. But I could feel very strongly that I should not be there.

I love a good party. I think most people do. I'm not talking about the sort of thing with music so loud you can't be heard. No, I'm talking about when a group of people comes together. You know, the camaraderie, the bonhomie, that comfortable feeling you get with a bunch of friends or family together. Maybe a few drinks, a lot of good laughs, perhaps a few songs. That sort of thing. That feeling of belonging.

There are times and places where things like that just seem to happen. My family has a part interest in an old cabin. It's way back in the woods up north. There's a river out the back, but the only access is a good half-mile from the road. A hundred-odd years ago, it was built as a hunting cabin, but it's really a family cabin now. Away from distractions of technology and things as everyday as electricity, you had to make your own fun. Parties up there were perfect.

That's not to say we didn't use it as a hunting cabin. I would come up to the cabin with Chuck, a good friend, and we got in some hunting for a few days before the family started to trickle in. Chuck used to be great fun at the family parties too. He loved coming up there, and since I'd known him since school, he was basically part of the family. Some nights when he was there, we'd be up all night and realize that just in time to stagger down the driveway to the road to watch the sun come up. Sadly, Chuck died about four years ago. Since then, I've never felt like going up to the cabin before the rest of the family arrives. Just too many memories of a life cut short too soon.

I guess I should point out that the cabin is a giant living room with lots of seating, two fireplaces, and a piano. There's a kitchen, big enough to feed the whole clan, off to one end. Beyond that, the rest of the cabin is in the form of screened-in porches around the outside. That's where we sleep most of the time.

If you've spent all your time in the city, you might think that a place like that would be spooky. You know, no electricity, just a screen between you and the woods. And it can get dark out there at night. Honestly, though, that's not the case. Even when I was young, I felt that the forest was, for want of a better word, welcoming. I'm not saying I didn't see some strange things out there some nights—I did—but the forest never gave me any reason to fear it.

The cabin itself, well, I've seldom felt it was a scary place, but there have been some things that have unsettled me. Like, one night, I was sleeping on the porch near one of the screen doors. I don't know what woke me, but I thought I heard footfalls on the leaf-covered ground outside. As I said, the forest has never bothered me. I just figured someone had gotten up for a stroll in the middle of the night. It was a beautiful night, with a full moon and only a few clouds.

When I heard the porch steps creak and then the screen door squeak, I was sure. I raised my head to see who it was. There was no one. There's no way anyone could have come in and moved fast enough for me not to have seen them. I was right by the door. Just couldn't happen.

I swear my mouth dropped open. My eyes were trying to look everywhere at once. The shivers that ran down my spine had nothing to do with the cool night air. I'd heard the door. I knew I had. So where was …?

Then the rational part of me woke and kicked in. I'd been dreaming. That was the reason, a convincing and quite lucid dream, but just a dream. Grinning sheepishly at myself and hoping no one else was awake to see me, I lay back down and drifted off. Another mystery solved.

Well, that's what I thought. See, the thing is, the cabin is so old, and the family is so extended that we decided it was time to have a meeting. Get everyone from all four branches of the family together and make plans for the place. After a hundred-plus years, you have to start thinking about a bit of maintenance and the like.

We met in the living room. The kids had been put to bed, out on the porch. I wasn't the only one with a beer to hand. The fire was blazing away, bouncing shadows off the walls. The deer heads mounted on the walls almost seemed to move in the flickering firelight.

We'd covered all the practical stuff, and the conversation had started to wane a bit when someone mentioned something about weirdness. I don't know who started it, but after some self-conscious glances and throat-clearing, it all started to come out. I wasn't the only one to have heard the door. It had happened to other people too. I shivered again. Now it was much harder to write it off as a dream. You don't share dreams just because you sleep in the same place. Do you?

Then there were the other stories. Each one brought back a memory for me—things I'd seen and felt but pushed to the back of my mind. After all, it's a modern world. A half-hour drive gets you to the city. Civilization! You get in the car, you drive down the road, and the bright lights and sounds move odd thoughts out of your head.

But that night, sitting together by the light of the fire, with the dark of the forest outside, I couldn't hide from my memories. There were things I'd experienced, and now others were telling me they'd experienced the same.

There was the Old Man in the chair. You'd be in the living room late at night, with a group, and happen to look at the chair by the kitchen door. An older man would be sitting in it. The details of him were never clear. Just the feeling he was old. You'd turn away, talk to someone before you realized he didn't fit. Everyone who was supposed to be here was already accounted for. Then you'd snap your head back, but of course the chair would be empty. We all stopped talking that night, slowly turning together to the chair by the kitchen door. It was empty. Of course.

That was the way things happened. You'd all be having fun. Something would catch your attention, but only briefly. By the time you realized it was odd, it was too late. Like when a perfect night was going on. Everyone would be talking, laughing, shouting, and then someone would start to play a bit of music on the piano. That wasn't unusual, so you'd just enjoy the sound and carry on. Then someone would turn to speak to the piano player, and the music would stop because there'd be no one there.

Then someone else mentioned the "party." As I said, we slept out on the porches. The main living room was usually empty at night. Yet, a couple of people claimed they'd heard party noises from the living room when everyone had been out sleeping. I looked around. There was a lot of nodding going on. I nodded too. It was a couple of years ago, and I'd put it down as another dream, but maybe …

I'd been one of the last to turn in that night. Being one of the unmarried males in the group, I was relegated to a couch under one of the living room windows way down in the darkest corner of the back porch. I have no idea when I finally got to the couch, but I know I was one of the last to leave the living room. When you're in your early twenties, you feel you can party all night, but exhaustion catches up with you, even at that age. I just fell on the couch and was out almost before I had time to pull the covers over myself.

Sometime later—I have no idea when I was awakened—there was a lot of noise coming from the living room. Laughter, voices, music! It sounded like another good party had got going while I was asleep. Oddly, no matter how much I strained, I couldn't make out what they were talking about. The voices were loud enough, but they just seemed to run together incoherently. It was the same with the music. I heard music, but I couldn't isolate the melody. I shook my head. That didn't help.

Well, enough of this anyway. If some of the others were going to get up in the middle of the night and restart the party, I should join them. I sat up, still trying to shake the sleep out of my head and glanced through the living room window.

Silence. And blackness. The living room was dark and empty. There was no noise. I was sitting up, half off the couch. I knew I'd heard a party, but there was nothing. I froze.

I became aware that there was something. I felt as if I was being watched. The more I looked into the living room, the worse the feeling got. My heart was thumping hard, battering my rib cage. I swear, if there'd been the slightest sound at that point, it would have burst. There was nothing I could see, but that feeling would not go away. Something in the living room was watching me.

I slowly lowered my head. As my eyes slipped below the windowsill, the feeling vanished. Everything seemed normal again. I was about to raise my head and look back into the living room, but something stopped me. Sleep seemed to be much more important. I slipped back under the covers and was almost instantly asleep again.

The next morning, I just assumed it was a dream. I even felt a bit sheepish about the whole getting scared thing. After all, I was a man in his early twenties. Bad dreams are not the sort of thing someone like that shares with others. But, now, some of the others reported the same feelings, the same sounds, the same experience. Subtly I moved my chair a little closer to the fire.

The topic of conversation moved on to new fields. More beer was drunk, more jokes told. The atmosphere lightened again, and I put those stories behind me once more. My aunt started on one of her admittedly hilarious, long, rambling tales. I settled in my chair and gave her my full attention.

As the night wore on, the remaining people began drifting out to the porch. That's the way it goes. There's no sudden end to an evening in the cabin, just a drifting away till a little core group is left sitting by the embers of the fire. There were three of us left when we discovered we'd finally been able to exceed the porches' sleeping capacity. With all four families in the cabin, we'd entirely run out of space. There were two spots left out on the porch, and as the other two were a couple, I offered to sleep in the living room and give them the spots. I dragged a blow-up mattress in from my car. With my blanket and a couple of cushions from a sofa, I'd be snug by the fireplace.

I don't know when I woke up, but I do know why. There was a party in full swing in the living room. The noise, singing, and laughing woke me. I leaped from my mattress. The room was empty, dark, and still. There was no party. I was standing alone in an empty room.

Okay. A dream again? Well, we'd been talking about all this before, so it might be. I remained standing for a minute or two. I wanted to make sure, to myself, that I was awake. I was sure I was, but what I couldn't shake was the tension in the air, the feeling that something was not right. The only way I can describe it is a feeling that there was something in that room that shouldn't have been there. There was nothing I could see, in the dim light of the moon, or hear, yet the tension wouldn't leave me.

Assuming I was getting wound up because of the earlier conversation, I slowly lowered myself back to my mattress. I looked around one more time and laid my head on the cushion. Nothing there! I closed my eyes.

Only to instantly flick them open again as the noise resumed. Once my eyes opened, the noise stopped. This was ridiculous. This was some weird dream, and I hadn't had that much to drink. I looked around again. Nothing moving, nothing happening. The feeling that something was out of place wouldn't shift, though. I felt my muscles tense, my body straining against the sentiment. But there was nothing. I forced my body to relax.

I closed my eyes. The party noise was back. I opened them. Nothing! No noise, nothing. Was I losing my mind? Was I dreaming? What was going on here?

I closed my eyes again. The noise came back. I was exhausted, dog-tired. I did something I can't really explain, even to this day. I pulled the covers over my head, determined to ignore the noise. I'd sleep and figure it out tomorrow.

A hand touched my arm. A voice, clear and recognizable, spoke my name in my ear.

I sat up again with a jolt. The noise stopped, but it didn't matter anymore. I stood, grabbed my mattress and blanket, and left the room. I slept the rest of the night outside, under the stars. There was no way I could sleep in that room. It wasn't my place.

I'd recognized the voice. I'd have recognized it anywhere. It was Chuck. I just hope he saves a spot at that party for me when my time comes.

Conclusion

Are you feeling unsettled? The world may not be as simple as we thought. There are things out there that make you wonder. People report experiences that leave you with that sense of wonder and fear. What did they experience? What actually went on? What is behind the stories people told us? Is the world really a much more mysterious place than we think?

I hope so. Mystery is what makes life interesting. It is the driver of both fear and exploration. Lovecraft may have been right about the fear of the unknown, but the world would be a much duller place without mystery. Like the ones you've read, mysteries are great because they remind us we don't know everything. Of course, mysteries can be a little more uncomfortable if you are in the middle of one.

So what about those red lights in the sky I mentioned before? Well, that is a mystery I can explain. I was living in China at the time, working at a university in south China. My wife and I watched the red lights floating past outside the campus with that same sense of wonder and perhaps a little fear. It took us a few minutes, but then we realized what they were. It was a festival in China that night, and the red lights were just paper lanterns with candles in them.

In some ways, knowing that took some of the mystery out of the world. Finding the answer, while a relief, did bring us back to a mundane reality. However, it does not take away the experience. I will always remember the feeling of wonder when we watched the lights glide by, the sense of mystery. I'm glad I had the experience and, to a degree, relieved that we could explain it. Strangely, I'm also happy I can't explain the wardrobe, or at least I am now nearly twenty years later. It's nice to have a mystery. It's nice to know the world can't be explained all the time.

That doesn't mean I'd like to experience the same things that the people who sent in their stories did. The stories in this book seem like things best avoided. Some things in the world seem too weird, too scary, and too out of this world for me. Scratching in the wardrobe is one thing, meeting a strange creature alone in the woods is quite another.

Dave Hann

Printed in Great Britain
by Amazon

29426018R00071